THIS
LIFE PURPOSE
PLAYBOOK
BELONGS TO

NAME

I, _____, commit to celebrating myself and following

this LIFE PURPOSE PLAYBOOK system for the next 6 months.

Above all, I commit to honoring myself and my days throughout this journey and forever after.

If lost, please call or email me at _____

LIFE PURPOSE PLAYBOOK

Book design by Theresa McNeilly
www.theresamcneilly.com
Inside mandala design by Gina Miranda
www.GinaMirandaArt.com

My Purpose Discovery Formula™ and My Life Intention
Matrix™ are adapted from the concept of Unique
Ability®, which is created and owned by The Strategic
Coach, Inc.

Original publication date October 2015
Printed by www.printingicon.com
Version 1.1
ISBN-13: 978-1518605789
ISBN-10: 1518605788

To re-order your LIFE PURPOSE PLAYBOOK,
or to learn about our workshops or video programs,
visit us at **www.lifepurposeplaybook.com**

TABLE OF CONTENTS

DEDICATION

This book is dedicated to my beautiful
mother, Judite, who has always encouraged
me to follow my dreams! She has been my
angel and my rock, loving me unconditionally
all of these years.

A special thank you to this earth angel,
Theresa McNeilly. Her skills as an
Industrial Designer, coupled with her
own transformative awakening, are fully
expressed in the book's design. Every detail
has been collaborated and designed with
meaning and intent. Theresa, because of
you, this book is glowing with love and light.
Always know that I love you and I see you.

Another special thank you to my early
mentors, Tony Robbins and Wayne Dyer.
Both have inspired me to dream powerfully
and to believe!

A PERSONAL MESSAGE FROM THE CREATOR

At a young age, I learned one of the most valuable lessons of my life: dedicating myself to personal growth AND TAKING THE TIME TO DO THE EXERCISES. Many people read or go to courses & seminars but never stop to actually do the exercises that are suggested. I believe that TRANSFORMATION comes from DOING.

I created this LIFE PURPOSE PLAYBOOK because I want to help others to STOP AND DO the self-discovery exercises in a fun & interactive way. I've been goal setting & daily planning for over 20 years now, yet I haven't been able to find the perfect daily planner to support my system. So I decided to CREATE ONE!

My wish is that this book becomes a tool to support YOUR personal development journey and create transformation for you as well. It was designed to inspire you to dream, to act, and to taste life with enriched experiences, created by YOU.

As we all awaken into our purpose, we become capable of creating extraordinary positive changes for the greater good of humanity.

Enjoy your journey!
With love & gratitude,

Judy Machado-Duque
www.justJUDY.ca

P.S. 5% of all profits from this book are donated to Mercy For Animals, a non-profit organization, who have influenced me to live more compassionately.

5 STEPS TO MAXIMIZE THIS LIFE PURPOSE PLAYBOOK

Are you chronically distracted by things like social media and multi-tasking? This LIFE PURPOSE PLAY BOOK is designed to keep you focused and to record everything that you would like to manifest into your life. Applying this simple system will allow you to become passionate, organized and focused, every day. It's time to **STEP INTO THE WORLD** with your personal gifts. It's time to **MAKE A DIFFERENCE!**

Get into the habit of carrying your LIFE PURPOSE PLAYBOOK with you everywhere you go, so that you can be inspired and living on purpose all the time.

This LIFE PURPOSE PLAYBOOK was not designed for a specific calendar year. This way, you can begin your journey anytime of the year and at any point in the month! It was designed to last you **6 months**, light and thin enough to be able to carry with you everywhere you go. You and I both know that you wouldn't carry around a book twice as thick as this! Once you've completed this book, you can order another one at **www.lifepurposeplaybook.com** There is enormous value in recreating your goals more then once a year. Whatever we focus on grows!

This book is your life in LIVING COLOR. It has been printed purposefully in black and white so that you can add color and your personal flair to each page. Get yourself a pack of PENCIL CRAYONS and enjoy coloring this entire book including the quote pages. Start by coloring the mandala flower on the first page of this LIFE PURPOSE PLAYBOOK. This will help to activate your right brain, your creativity. This is a great exercise to do BEFORE you start working on your goals. Make it personal, use your favorite colors, then take a selfie with it (or one of your colored quote sheets) and share with us and our community at **www.lifepurposeplaybook.com**

If you want to start right away on your daily planner, then skip to page 56 to begin from there. But, make sure to take the time to complete all of the activities in this LIFE PURPOSE PLAYBOOK. A solid foundation is the key to the success of this system. It may take you some time to complete them all, and that's OK. Be patient with yourself and your journey, and know that you're taking the time for yourself to uncover your purpose and passions.

As a certified Coach and Practitioner of NLP (Neuro Linguistic Programming), I've created an interactive video guide to help you through each of the activities. Along with additional tools to help overcome procrastination. Visit **www.lifepurposeplaybook.com** to order and to enhance this journey for you.

6 As you experience this journey of time and life mastery, please share with us your personal stories at **www.lifepurposeplaybook.com**. Enjoy this exhilarating experience!

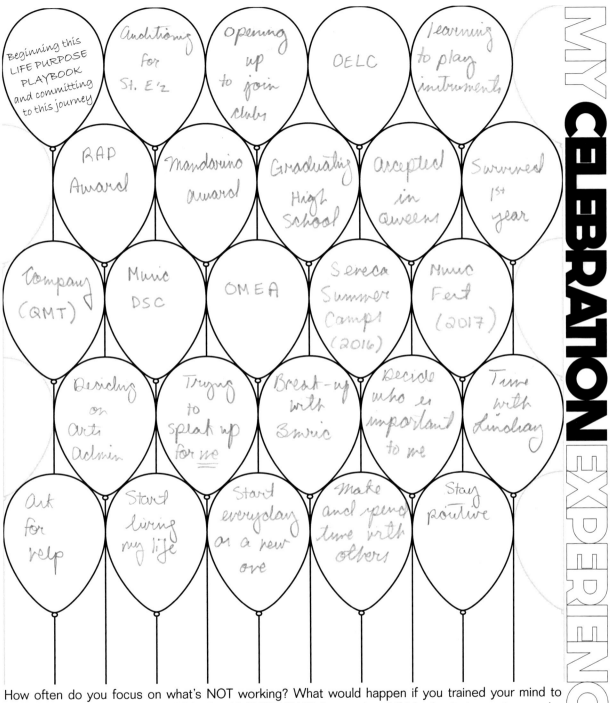

Beginning this LIFE PURPOSE PLAYBOOK and committing to this journey

Auditioning for St. E'z

Opening up to join clubs

OELC

learning to play instruments

RAP Award

Mandarino award

Graduating High School

accepted in Queens

Survived 1st year

Company (QMT)

Music DSC

OMEA

Seneca Summer Camp (2016)

Music Fest (2017)

Deciding on Arts Admin

Trying to speak up for me

Break-up with 3 music

Decide who is important to me

Time with Lindsay

Art for relp

Start living my life

Start everyday as a new one

make and spend time with others

Stay positive

How often do you focus on what's NOT working? What would happen if you trained your mind to acknowledge and CELEBRATE what IS WORKING? Image the shift! Let's start your journey by focusing on the many successes in your life. First, take a deep breath and relax. Now, in the SPACE above, create a list of 24 achievements in your life that you are most proud of. These can be small AND big achievements. Keep writing and don't stop. Although 24 may seem like a lot, keep pushing through to find those jewels. Let the ideas come to you quickly and take the time to smile as you remember them all!

WHEN YOUR LIFE IS ON COURSE WITH ITS **PURPOSE**

YOU ARE YOUR MOST **POWERFUL**

OPRAH WINFREY

THIS LIFE PURPOSE PLAYBOOK IS DIVIDED INTO 2 PARTS:

PART 1 PAGES 11-25

DISCOVER MY PURPOSE

WHERE THE **MAGIC** HAPPENS

LIVE MY LIFE ON PURPOSE

PART 2 PAGES 26-271

What is your **WHY**?
What is it that **INSPIRES** you?
What is your **REASON** for wanting more in your life?

Your **WHY** is what fuels your passion and keeps you committed and living on purpose.

A simple system to keep you excited and focused on your purpose everyday.

1. MY DAILY PAGE PLATFORM™
2. MY WEEKLY CHECK-IN™

Feel free to begin right away with this daily system even before you complete the activities from PART 1. But make sure to take the time, soon, to complete all of them. This will ensure you spend your days aligned with your purpose.

This journey you are about to begin is all about planning ahead, while staying present to all of the ABUNDANCE in your life RIGHT NOW. The source of all ABUNDANCE is within you. To awaken this ABUNDANCE, notice everything around you that is ABUNDANCE. The roof over your head, the food you eat, the sunshine, your shoes, the local transportation system. The way to attract more ABUNDANCE into your life is to live with the feeling that you are already ABUNDANT. As you go through this book and create goals, stay present to those feelings of ABUNDANCE so that you create even more.

Remember to use colored pens and pencil crayons as much as possible throughout this
LIFE PURPOSE PLAYBOOK, **to awaken your creative juices!**

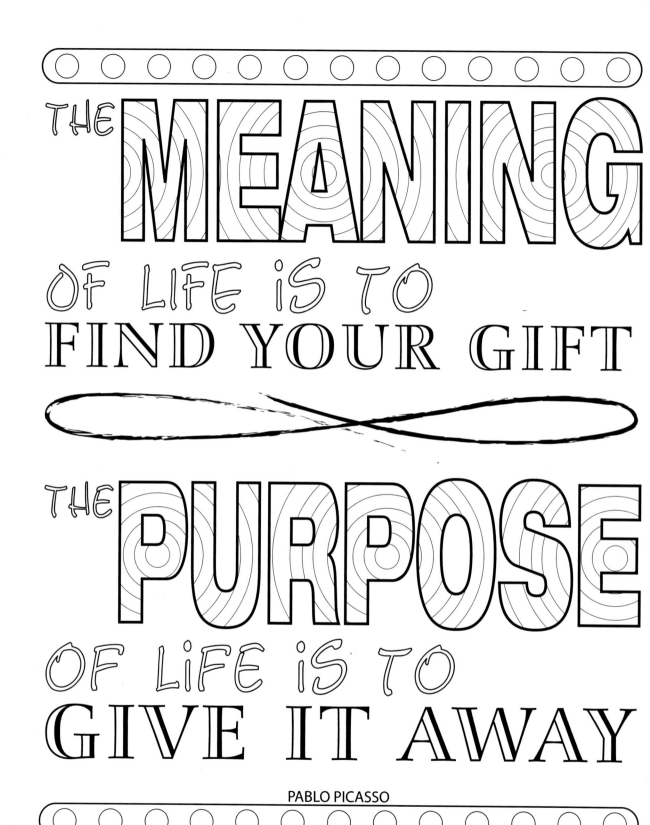

THE **MEANING** OF LIFE IS TO FIND YOUR GIFT

THE **PURPOSE** OF LIFE IS TO GIVE IT AWAY

PABLO PICASSO

Do you feel a little confused or unclear about your PURPOSE in life? Do you want to be doing more with your life? Perhaps even something that will help to create a positive impact on the world? In the SPACE below, follow the steps to uncover your PURPOSE.

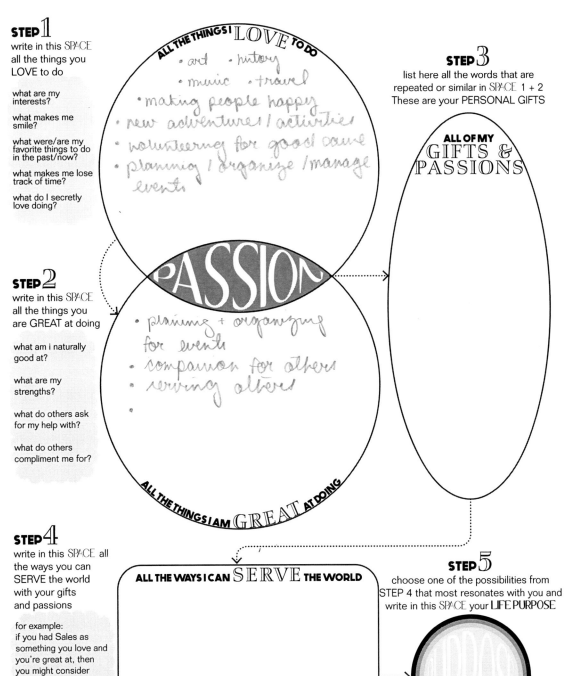

STEP 1
write in this SPACE all the things you LOVE to do

what are my interests?

what makes me smile?

what were/are my favorite things to do in the past/now?

what makes me lose track of time?

what do I secretly love doing?

ALL THE THINGS I LOVE TO DO
- art   • history
- music   • travel
- making people happy
- new adventures / activities
- volunteering for good cause
- planning / organize / manage events

STEP 3
list here all the words that are repeated or similar in SPACE 1 + 2 These are your PERSONAL GIFTS

ALL OF MY GIFTS & PASSIONS

PASSION

STEP 2
write in this SPACE all the things you are GREAT at doing

what am i naturally good at?

what are my strengths?

what do others ask for my help with?

what do others compliment me for?

- planning + organizing for events
- companion for others
- serving others
-

ALL THE THINGS I AM GREAT AT DOING

STEP 4
write in this SPACE all the ways you can SERVE the world with your gifts and passions

for example:
if you had Sales as something you love and you're great at, then you might consider these possibilities:
- sales consultant
- work for a company in their sales department
- teach sales

ALL THE WAYS I CAN SERVE THE WORLD

STEP 5
choose one of the possibilities from STEP 4 that most resonates with you and write in this SPACE your LIFE PURPOSE

PURPOSE

IT'S NOT HARD TO MAKE DECISIONS ONCE YOU KNOW WHAT YOUR VALUES ARE

ROY E. DISNEY

VALUES give us purpose and direction. Your personal VALUES are a central part of who you are, and who you want to be. They should determine your priorities and can become the measures you use to determine if your life is turning out the way you want it to. They are unique and important to you. As we live in integrity with our VALUES, we no longer depend on external recognition or approval.

When we align our actions with our VALUES on a daily basis, we feel more fulfilled. When we don't align with our VALUES, we feel inauthentic and we become less excited about life.

For example, if you VALUE FAMILY, but you work a 60 hour week, will you feel fulfilled and happy? And if you VALUE LOVE, yet you surround yourself with friends who are always judging others and creating drama, are you likely to feel conflict?

In these types of situations, understanding your VALUES can really help.

When you know your own VALUES, you can use them to create boundaries, manage your time and make decisions about how to live your life.

You can then answer questions like these with more clarity:

What line of work would most fulfill me?

Should I date this person?

Should I compromise, or stay firm in my position?

Should I speak up?

STEP 1 Circle the top 5 VALUES that most **RESONATE** with you. Feel free to add any others.

Authenticity Achievement Adventure Beauty
Challenge Comfort Courage Creativity Curiosity Education
Empowerment Environment Family Financial-Freedom Fitness Balance
Gratitude Love Friendship Service Health Honesty Independence Inner-Peace
Integrity Intelligence Intimacy Joy Leadership Learning Motivation Passion
Compassion Credibility Empathy Humor Recreation Peace Performance
Personal-Growth Play Productivity Reliability Respect Security
Spirituality Success Time-Freedom Variety

STEP 2 In the SPACE below, list your top 5 VALUES in ORDER OF IMPORTANCE to you.

MY TOP 5 VALUES

Now that you have clarified your purpose, you can create a clear LIFE INTENTION.

This concept is similar to a mission statement, a one or two sentence statement describing the reason you exist. But it is written as an INTENTION. This will provide clarity and give you a sense of purpose. It gives you permission to say NO to things that are distractions. Your LIFE INTENTION may change over time, as you acquire more life experiences and skills.

What is your LIFE INTENTION? What can you do with your life to become fulfilled, to create value for others, to help the greater good of humanity?

The more you clarify what it is you want, the more you will be able to make decisions about priorities in your life. You may then start to attract people, opportunities, circumstances and events into your life to make it happen.

Your LIFE INTENTION should be easily said by you and should be **RECOGNIZABLY YOURS.**

STEP 1
Circle 1-4 ACTION words within the SPACE below.
Choose words that most resonate and inspire you! Feel free to add any others.

Accomplish
Express Master Acquire Connect Measure
Construct Facilitate Restore Administrate Adopt
Co-ordinate Foster Motivate Safeguard Counsel Advise
Create Gather Negotiate Save Affect Generate Nurture Sell
Defend Give Serve Organize Share Deliver Guide Analyze
Demonstrate Heal Appreciate Help Perform Spread Assist
Discover Host Play Support Practice Believe Distribute Illuminate
Implement Prepare Dream Improve Present Build Drive Produce
Teach Educate Inform Progress Team Cause Inspire Touch Change
Embrace Integrate Promote Empower Translate Encourage
Pursue Travel Engage Collect Engineer Reclaim Enhance
Coach Launch Reduce Enlighten Lead Refine Validate
Communicate Enlist Learn Reflect Value Enliven
Light Volunteer Entertain Love Write
Evaluate Release Manage Explore
Manifest

STEP 2

In the SPACE below, write **WHAT** services you would like to be offering in life.

For example:
coach, engineer, create systems, public speaking, workshops

STEP 3

In the SPACE below, write to **WHOM** you would like to offer your services.

For example:
children, businesses, entrepreneurs, animals or people in general.

STEP 4

Transfer the **ACTION** words you selected from STEP 1 into this SPACE above. This becomes the VALUE you create for others in your life.

For example:
promote, empower, entertain, enlighten, alive

STEP 5

In this SPACE above, transfer any of YOUR TOP 5 VALUES (page 13) that align with your purpose.

For example:
time freedom, balance

STEP 6

In the SPACE below, combine STEPS 2, 3, 4 and 5 to complete **YOUR** LIFE INTENTION.

Here is an example.....My LIFE INTENTION is to empower entrepreneurs, to create balance and become enlightened & alive through interactive workshops.

You did it! Congratulations!

LIVE EVERY DAY WITH **INTENTION** AND WATCH YOUR LIFE TRANSFORM!

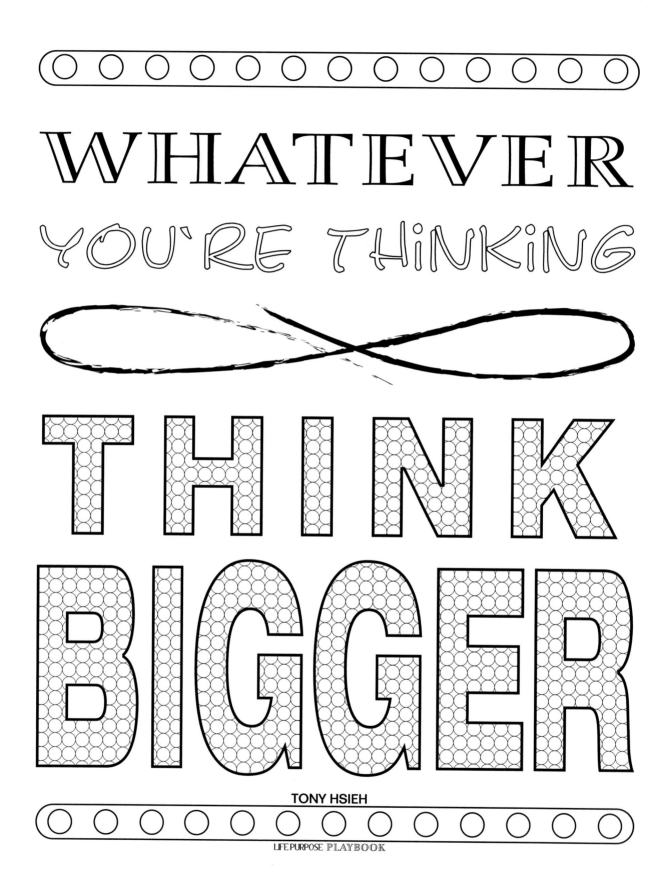

WHATEVER

YOU'RE THINKING

THINK BIGGER

TONY HSIEH

If you don't know where you are going, you will end up exactly there! Now that you have a clear LIFE INTENTION, It's time to get specific on all your DREAMS.

In this exercise, you will write your goals starting with the words **I AM** (then write your goal). This will create BELIEF in the present moment so that you BECOME THE GOAL.

For example:
"**I AM** spending my days working from my modern home office as a journalist, creating value for others".
"**I HAVE** an abundant & generous mindset".

These **I AM** or **I HAVE** statements become a command to the Universe to create instant belief and results.

This activity will help you to **BELIEVE** it before you see it. It will create the possibility for you that your DREAMS can become reality.

Take a deep breath. On the SPACE below, write down all of your DREAMS, big and small. Here are some questions you can use to help spark your imagination:

• Where is your DREAM home and what **EXACTLY** does it look like? Why do you want this home?
• Describe the way you spend your DREAM days?
• If you didn't have to work to earn money, what would you do?
• How would you **LOVE** to contribute to the world?
• What is everything you wish to **BE, DO** and **HAVE** in your life?

Don't stop writing until you fill this page! Write as fast as you can. Keep moving your pen & stay inspired. **MAGIC** happens when you write down your DREAMS.

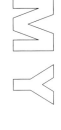

MY DREAM BUILDER™

17

Use these two pages to create your VISION BOARD! Cut and paste (or draw) pictures here that reflect your dreams and desires. Pictures are important to fuel your desires & attract your dreams. Look at these two pages, your VISION BOARD, every day. Close your eyes, every day, and SEE yourself in these images. Feel all of the feelings of having all of this goodness in your life. The Universe will give you exactly what you think about most of the time!

MY VISION BOARD™

18

MY VISION BOARD™

19

BALANCE
IS NOT SOMETHING YOU
FIND
IT'S SOMETHING YOU
CREATE

AUTHOR UNKNOWN

Sometimes, life gets so busy that we need to take a "bird's eye view" of our life. This allows us to see the big picture and get our life back into balance. The CIRCLE below contains 10 areas of your life. Your fulfillment in these areas are the key to balance and happiness.

STEP 1 Each life area is represented on a scale of 0-10. In the SPACE below, rate (by coloring) how satisfied and fulfilled you are currently with each area.

Rating: **0=dissatisfied 10=completely satisfied**

For example, it may be that you are a 6/10 on your health life area so you will color in that SPACE 0 to 6.

Once you have colored in each of the areas, you will see just how balanced or unbalanced your life is. If you have very high numbers on some and very low numbers on others, you may want to create focus on the areas of your life with the lower numbers.

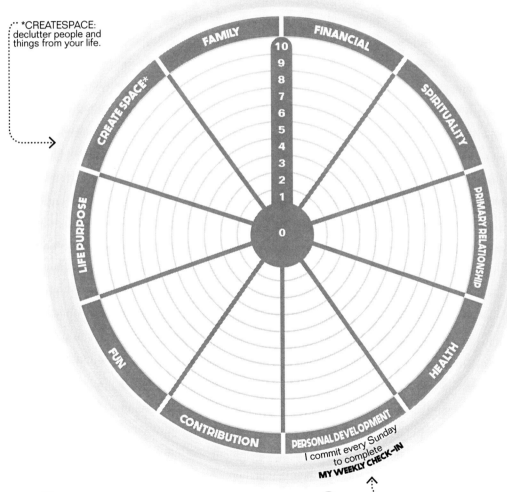

*CREATESPACE: declutter people and things from your life.

I commit every Sunday to complete
MY WEEKLY CHECK-IN

STEP 2 Decide which areas you would like to have more focus over the next year, and use a different color to **EXPAND** that focus.
Color in your desired score on a scale of 0-10 on where you want to be in that area of focus.

STEP 3 Once you have a colored picture indicating your **PRESENT** satisfaction with each area, and your **DESIRED** satisfaction, now you can set a commitment for each. This commitment will help to create focus for that area for the next year ahead. See example.

Now we can start to create some clear goals that align with your LIFE PURPOSE, LIFE INTENTION and DREAMS.

SMART is a tool and acronym to help to expand and track your GOALS. Let's imagine your general goal is to start taking yoga classes. By turning it into a SMART GOAL, it can be enhanced with depth and priority.

Follow the example below to practice turning your **GENERAL GOALS** into SMART GOALS.

	FOR EXAMPLE:	WRITE YOUR GOAL HERE:
What is your **AREA OF FOCUS?** (from MY CIRCLE OF LIFE EXPANDER™)	Health	
What is your **GENERAL GOAL?**	Start taking Yoga classes	
S Include SPECIFIC details. Who, what, where, when, which, why	Hot Yoga	
M Progress should be MEASURABLE. Include dates, dollars or other units. Clarify when the goal is to be completed.	1 hour class weekly for 3 months	
A Is the goal ACHIEVABLE and realistic? Are you giving yourself a reasonable amount of time to complete the goal? Do you really believe that you can accomplish this goal?	I will give myself 3 weeks to find a Yoga studio & begin classes January 11	
R Is this goal RELEVANT to YOUR life dreams & is it aligned with your LIFE INTENTION? Be sure not to take on other people's goals instead of your own.	Yes it is relevant because Yoga is one of MY personal interests and I want more focus on my health	
T How much TIME will it take to achieve the goal? This will set your subconscious mind into motion to begin working on your goal.	3 months starting Jan 11	
What is YOUR SMART GOAL?	I AM participating in a 1 hour hot Yoga class, weekly for 3 months starting Jan 11.	

22

This LIFE PURPOSE PLAYBOOK was designed to integrate all aspects of your life and not just your business or career. On the next page, each of the 10 life area's from MY CIRCLE OF LIFE EXPANDER™ (pg 21) are listed in chart form. Creating focus on all areas of your life will help to create balance and fulfillment.

There are **2 STEPS** to complete MY GOAL CHARTING SYSTEM™:

STEP 1

On the next page, under the column **MY ULTIMATE GOALS**, you will write all of your GOALS for each life area. Be sure to start each goal with **I AM** or **I HAVE**.

STEP 2

In the chart on the next page, under the column **MY 6 MONTH GOALS**, you will write all of your short-term goals.

For both steps above, be sure to take all of your DREAMS from MY DREAM BUILDER™ exercise (page 17), and include your 10 commitments (page 21, step 3).

TIP 1 ACT AS IF...
Begin right now to **act, live, be** the person you would be if you had already achieved your goal. The Universal Law Of Attraction works when we attach feeling to our goals.

TIP 2 LET GO OF ATTACHMENT...
Sometimes, we want to have a certain job or career, when in fact, the universe has better plans for us. This may only be understood in the future, looking backwards. That's why letting go is so important. **Letting go** is letting happiness in.

TIP 3 BE HAPPY NOW...
If you're attached to a specific outcome, such as a dream job or a specific home to buy, you may be creating for yourself a belief that only when those things happen will you be happy. Always remember that all the happiness you need can come from your **NOW**, the present moment. Don't get so focused on the goals and the results that you forget to find joy in the present.

Below is an example of how to complete MY GOAL CHARTING SYSTEM™ on the next 2 pages.

EXAMPLE

MY ULTIMATE GOALS (include feelings)	MY 6 MONTH GOALS
I am living financially free and in a space of accomplishment and self respect.	I set aside 5% of my income every month in a separate bank account for real estate investments.
I have a growing portfolio of real estate investment properties that are creating for me increased passive income every year.	I have read 3 best selling books on financial intelligence.

FINANCIAL

MY GOAL CHARTING SYSTEM™

24

FINANCIAL

SPIRITUALITY

PRIMARY RELATIONSHIP

HEALTH

PERSONAL DEVELOPMENT

MY ULTIMATE GOALS (include feelings)

MY 6 MONTH GOALS

MY ULTIMATE GOALS (include feelings)

MY 6 MONTH GOALS

FAMILY

CREATE SPACE

LIFE PURPOSE

FUN

CONTRIBUTION

MY IDEA & PROJECT MAGNIFIER™

Use this SPACE to write **ideas or projects** that are aligned with your LIFE INTENTION & GOALS. Keep adding as you think of these throughout your journey.

MY IDEA & PROJECT MAGNIFIER™

These
ideas & projects
should support
YOUR LIFE
INTENTION
& GOALS.

27

MY TO-DO CHECKLIST

28

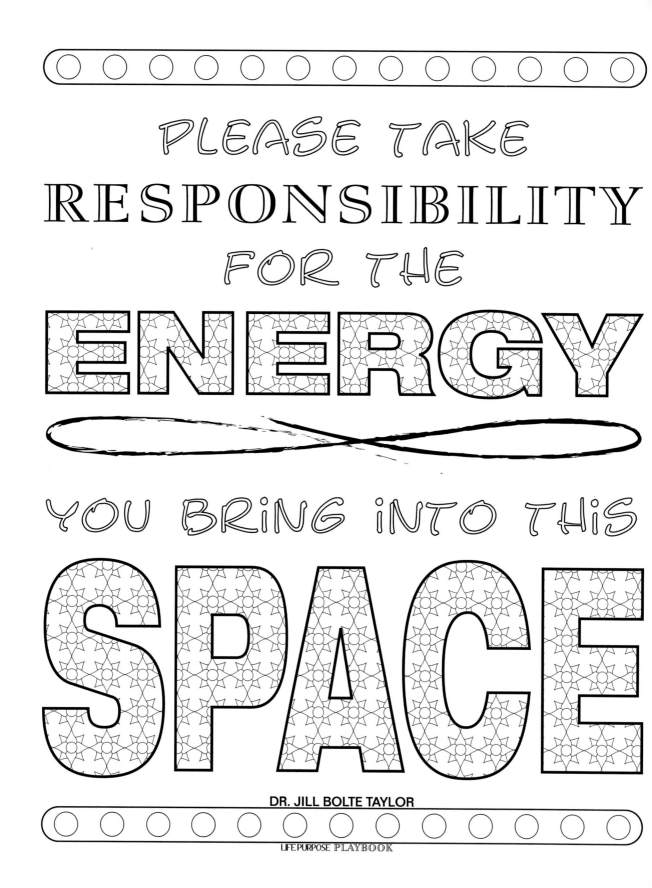

PLEASE TAKE RESPONSIBILITY FOR THE ENERGY YOU BRING INTO THIS SPACE

DR. JILL BOLTE TAYLOR

Use the following YEAR and MONTHLY CALENDARS to keep track of any appointments, plans and important dates (birthdays, project due dates, vacations, etc).

January

February

March

April

May

June

July

August

September

October

November

December

MONTH:

MONDAY	TUESDAY	WEDNESDAY	THURSDAY
4	5	6	7
11	12	13	14
18	19	20	21
25	26	27	28

MY MONTHLY PLANNER™

FRIDAY	SATURDAY	SUNDAY	NOTES
1	2	3	
8	9	10	
15	16	17	
22	23	24	
29	30		

MONTH:

MONDAY	TUESDAY	WEDNESDAY	THURSDAY

MY MONTHLY PLANNER™

34

FRIDAY	SATURDAY	SUNDAY	NOTES

MY MONTHLY PLANNER™

35

MONTH:

MONDAY	TUESDAY	WEDNESDAY	THURSDAY

36

FRIDAY	SATURDAY	SUNDAY	NOTES

MY MONTHLY PLANNER™

37

MONTH:

MONDAY	TUESDAY	WEDNESDAY	THURSDAY

FRIDAY	SATURDAY	SUNDAY	NOTES

MONTH:

MONDAY	TUESDAY	WEDNESDAY	THURSDAY

MY MONTHLY PLANNER™

40

FRIDAY	SATURDAY	SUNDAY	NOTES

MONTH:

MONDAY	TUESDAY	WEDNESDAY	THURSDAY

FRIDAY	SATURDAY	SUNDAY	NOTES

MY MONTHLY PLANNER™

MONTH:

MONDAY	TUESDAY	WEDNESDAY	THURSDAY

44

FRIDAY	SATURDAY	SUNDAY	NOTES

MONTH:

MONDAY	TUESDAY	WEDNESDAY	THURSDAY

FRIDAY	SATURDAY	SUNDAY	NOTES

MY MONTHLY PLANNER™

MONTH:

MONDAY	TUESDAY	WEDNESDAY	THURSDAY

FRIDAY	SATURDAY	SUNDAY	NOTES

MONTH:

MONDAY	TUESDAY	WEDNESDAY	THURSDAY

MY MONTHLY PLANNER™

50

FRIDAY	SATURDAY	SUNDAY	NOTES

MY MONTHLY PLANNER™

51

MONTH:

MY MONTHLY PLANNER™

MONDAY	TUESDAY	WEDNESDAY	THURSDAY

52

FRIDAY	SATURDAY	SUNDAY	NOTES

MONTH:

MONDAY	TUESDAY	WEDNESDAY	THURSDAY

MY MONTHLY PLANNER™

54

FRIDAY	SATURDAY	SUNDAY	NOTES

MY DAILY PAGE PLATFORM™ is THE TOOL that will create the framework for you to live your life on purpose EVERYDAY. It is your daily template designed to help you create time mastery. This will allow you to prioritize your projects and your life, as well as rejuvenate your body, mind and spirit.

Every morning take 5 minutes to plan your day with MY DAILY PAGE PLATFORM™. Then use this as a tool throughout the day to keep you focused and on purpose.

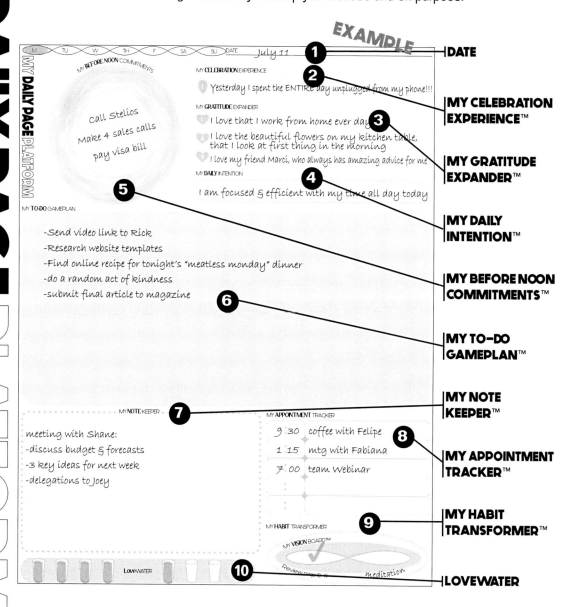

1 — DATE

2 — MY CELEBRATION EXPERIENCE™

3 — MY GRATITUDE EXPANDER™

4 — MY DAILY INTENTION™

5 — MY BEFORE NOON COMMITMENTS™

6 — MY TO-DO GAMEPLAN™

7 — MY NOTE KEEPER™

8 — MY APPOINTMENT TRACKER™

9 — MY HABIT TRANSFORMER™

10 — LOVEWATER

1 DATE
Fill in the date. Since this LIFE PURPOSE PLAYBOOK is flexible, you can begin your journey **ANY** day of the year!!!

2 MY CELEBRATION EXPERIENCE™
It's just as important to celebrate your successes as it is to achieve them! In this SPACE, write 1 of your successes from the day before! Too often we focus on what we didn't get done. Instead, LET'S FOCUS ON WHAT WE DID ACCOMPLISH! Beginning your day in a positive way will help to train your mind to look for and create more positive successes!

3 MY GRATITUDE EXPANDER™
Start each day with a GRATEFUL HEART. In this SPACE, write 3 things you are grateful for in that moment. This practice will forever change your life by turning what you HAVE into ENOUGH, and allowing you to attract more of what you're grateful for.

4 MY DAILY INTENTION™
Setting a daily intention is just as powerful as making a wish. It's like placing an order from the Universal menu of possibilities. In this SPACE, become the conscious creator of your experiences! Make sure your daily intention is positive and aligned with what it is you would like to have happen that day. Then look out for all the signs around you, delivering your wish. The Universe is always listening and sending us messages. The challenge is in slowing down and noticing. The more you notice these signs, the more you grow your abundance mindset.

5 MY BEFORE NOON COMMITMENTS™
In this SPACE, begin your morning by writing out your TOP 1-3 COMMITMENTS for the day. This is an EXCELLENT way to overcome PROCRASTINATION. Not only will you complete your most critical tasks BEFORE NOON, but you will feel so accomplished & empowered, which will create continued momentum throughout your day.

6 MY TO-DO GAMEPLAN™
In this SPACE, list all of your tasks and projects for the day. Remember to keep these focused on your goals. Don't confuse BEING BUSY with BEING PRODUCTIVE. Every time you complete one of your tasks, highlight it. The use of color will keep you focused on results. As you look at MY DAILY PAGE PLATFORM™ throughout the day, the more color you see, the more accomplished you will feel. You may also choose to prioritize the items on your TO-DO list, first thing in the morning.

7 MY NOTE KEEPER™
As you go about your day, on phone calls or working on your projects, use this SPACE to make notes.

8 MY APPOINTMENT TRACKER™
Use this SPACE to keep track of all appointments for the day. Make sure these appointments are ALL aligned with your goals & dreams. Don't waste time and energy on anything or anyone that is not adding to YOUR PRECIOUS ENERGY. Be critical with yourself, your time is valuable.

9 MY HABIT TRANSFORMER™
A habit is something we do regularly without consciously thinking about it. When we have goal-directed habits, we are progressing and building the change into our daily life.

There are 2 SPACES on MY HABIT TRANSFORMER™. One is for you to review MY VISION BOARD™ and spend at least a few minutes also to meditate and FEEL the emotions that come from LIVING those dreams. The other SPACE within MY HABIT TRANSFORMER™ is for you to add another empowering habit and of course, to follow through on that habit. Remember to check off once you've accomplished both habits for the day!

TIP: If you have a bad habit that you want to eliminate from your life, here is where you can keep yourself accountable. For example, if your bad habit is going to bed late every night, you can write "IN BED BY 10 PM" on MY HABIT TRANSFORMER™. Take your bad habits and convert them into a positive reminder.

10 LOVEWATER
Water is essential to keep you hydrated and in great energy so you can get more done! Most people say they don't drink enough water because they are too busy to remember. So here is a reminder to keep drinking throughout the day! With every glass you drink, color in one of the glass images on the page. This way you can track your progress and feel accomplished! Don't forget to LOVE your water!

This is THE MOST IMPORTANT STEP to living your life on purpose. It will create an opportunity to transform your next week ahead. Imagine the possibility of reaching your goals & dreams! If you don't take time to strategically review your goals and schedule some next steps into your daily routine, then "life will get in the way" and you'll end up "too busy".

Set aside at least 15-30 minutes every Sunday (or Monday morning) to do this. Making this weekly commitment can, over time, create MASSIVE TRANSFORMATION in your life.

TIP: Choose a physical SPACE that makes you feel good. Maybe it's in your favorite coffee shop or somewhere cozy in your home? Next, get your favorite drink (a special tea, or coffee?) and have this with you to enhance this weekly EXPERIENCE. Maybe even some food or some treats. This is important so that each week you look forward to this EXPERIENCE. You're taking time to plan out your future, so make sure you stay committed to this step, and always make it as enjoyable as possible.

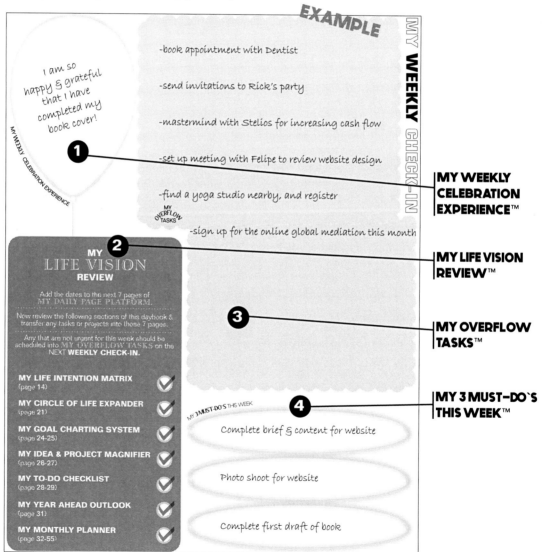

EXAMPLE

I am so happy & grateful that I have completed my book cover!

MY WEEKLY CELEBRATION EXPERIENCE

-book appointment with Dentist

-send invitations to Rick's party

-mastermind with Stelios for increasing cash flow

-set up meeting with Felipe to review website design

1

-find a yoga studio nearby, and register

MY OVERFLOW TASKS

-sign up for the online global mediation this month

2

MY WEEKLY CHECK-IN

MY
LIFE VISION
REVIEW

Add the dates to the next 7 pages of
MY DAILY PAGE PLATFORM.

Now review the following sections of this daybook &
transfer any tasks or projects into those 7 pages.

Any that are not urgent for this week should be
scheduled into MY OVERFLOW TASKS on the
NEXT WEEKLY CHECK-IN.

MY LIFE INTENTION MATRIX
(page 14)

MY CIRCLE OF LIFE EXPANDER
(page 21)

MY GOAL CHARTING SYSTEM
(page 24-25)

MY IDEA & PROJECT MAGNIFIER
(page 26-27)

MY TO-DO CHECKLIST
(page 28-29)

MY YEAR AHEAD OUTLOOK
(page 31)

MY MONTHLY PLANNER
(page 32-55)

3

4

MY 3 MUST-DO'S THIS WEEK

Complete brief & content for website

Photo shoot for website

Complete first draft of book

MY WEEKLY
CELEBRATION
EXPERIENCE™

MY LIFE VISION
REVIEW™

MY OVERFLOW
TASKS™

MY 3 MUST-DO`S
THIS WEEK™

Follow through and complete:

MY WEEKLY CHECK-IN™

Plan your next week ahead with:

MY DAILY PAGE PLATFORM™

(Monday to Sunday)
and begin to add tasks & projects to each of the 7 days, selecting which days are more appropriate for those tasks.

1 MY WEEKLY CELEBRATION EXPERIENCE™

As already suggested throughout this LIFE PURPOSE PLAYBOOK, focusing on your accomplishments will attract more goodness into your life. In this SPACE, you will be listing the MOST EXCITING accomplishment(s) from the past week. This way, you'll start off MY WEEKLY CHECK-IN™ in a positive state. Stay consistent with this empowering exercise and have fun along the way!

3 MY OVERFLOW TASKS™

Throughout the week, use this SPACE, to keep adding other tasks, projects or things to be completed next week. As well, any tasks that were not completed the week before can be transferred here. Then, next Sunday, when you review your weekly check-in, you can drop these into one of the next 7 days so that you create a commitment.

2 MY LIFE VISION REVIEW™

This section has been designed for you to refer back to your goals, as you plan your week ahead. In this SPACE, make sure to add a check mark next each section once reviewed. This weekly process will allow you to always remain focused on your goals & dreams. It will also create an opportunity to re-prioritize any ideas, tasks, projects and priorities into the next 7 days (Monday to Sunday) of MY DAILY PAGE PLATFORM™.

4 MY 3 MUST-DO'S THIS WEEK™

Use this SPACE to clarify 3 priorities that must be accomplished in order to keep progressing toward your goals.

59

IT'S NEVER BEEN EASIER
to share your
ideas &
passions
WITH THE WORLD

PETER DIAMANDIS

SUCCESS

is

FOUND

in your

daily
routine

JOHN C MAXWELL

M   TU   W   TH   F   SA   SU   DATE _____

MY DAILY PAGE PLATFORM™

MY *BEFORE NOON* COMMITMENTS™

am

MY *CELEBRATION* EXPERIENCE™

MY *GRATITUDE* EXPANDER™

MY *DAILY* INTENTION™

MY *TO-DO* GAMEPLAN™

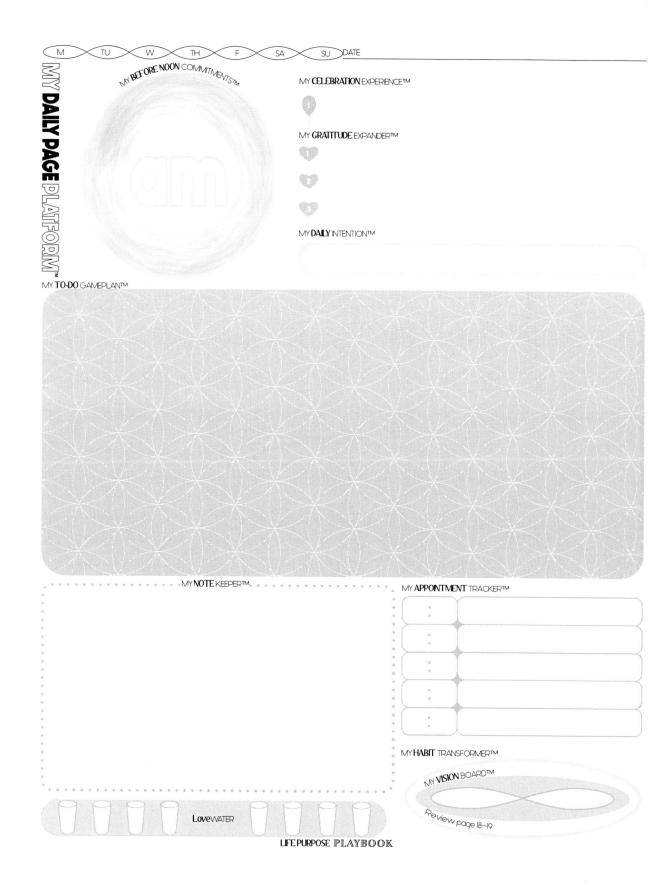

MY *NOTE* KEEPER™

MY *APPOINTMENT* TRACKER™

MY *HABIT* TRANSFORMER™

MY *VISION* BOARD™

Review page 18-19

Love WATER

LIFE PURPOSE PLAYBOOK

DATE _____

| M | TU | W | TH | F | SA | SU |

MY **CELEBRATION** EXPERIENCE™

MY **GRATITUDE** EXPANDER™

MY **DAILY** INTENTION™

MY **BEFORE NOON** COMMITMENTS™

MY **DAILY PAGE** PLATFORM™

MY **TO-DO** GAMEPLAN™

MY **APPOINTMENT** TRACKER™

MY **NOTE** KEEPER™

MY **HABIT** TRANSFORMER™

MY **VISION** BOARD™

Review page 18–19

Love WATER

LIFE PURPOSE PLAYBOOK

M TU W TH F SA SU DATE

MY **DAILY PAGE** PLATFORM™

MY **BEFORE NOON** COMMITMENTS™

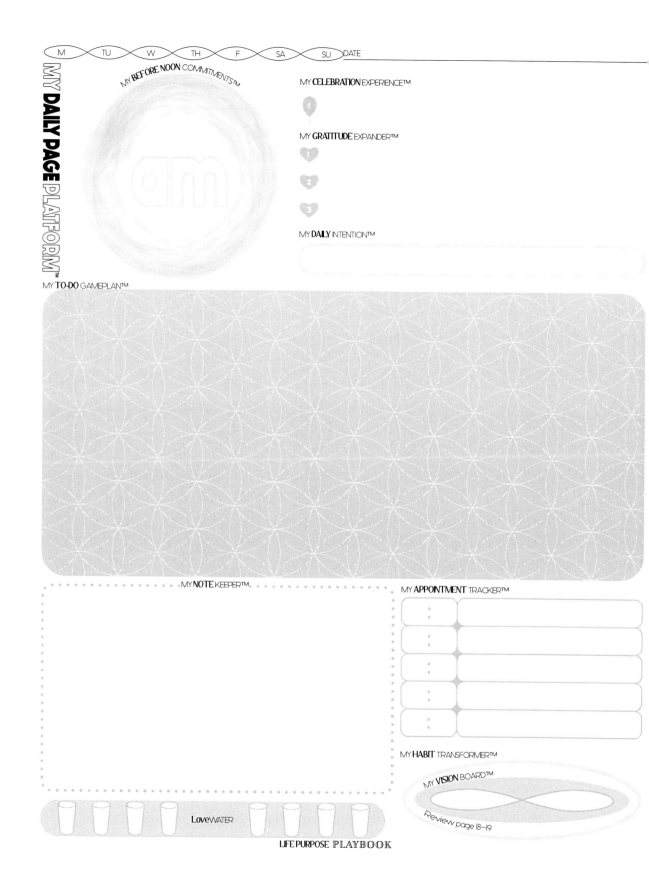

MY **CELEBRATION** EXPERIENCE™

MY **GRATITUDE** EXPANDER™

MY **DAILY** INTENTION™

MY **TO-DO** GAMEPLAN™

MY **NOTE** KEEPER™

MY **APPOINTMENT** TRACKER™

MY **HABIT** TRANSFORMER™

MY **VISION** BOARD™

Review page 18–19

Love WATER

LIFE PURPOSE PLAYBOOK

DATE _____ | M | TU | W | TH | F | SA | SU |

MY **CELEBRATION** EXPERIENCE™

MY **BEFORE NOON** COMMITMENTS™

MY **GRATITUDE** EXPANDER™

MY **DAILY** INTENTION™

MY **TO-DO** GAMEPLAN™

MY **APPOINTMENT** TRACKER™

MY **NOTE** KEEPER™

MY **HABIT** TRANSFORMER™

MY **VISION** BOARD™

Review page 18–19

Love WATER

LIFE PURPOSE PLAYBOOK

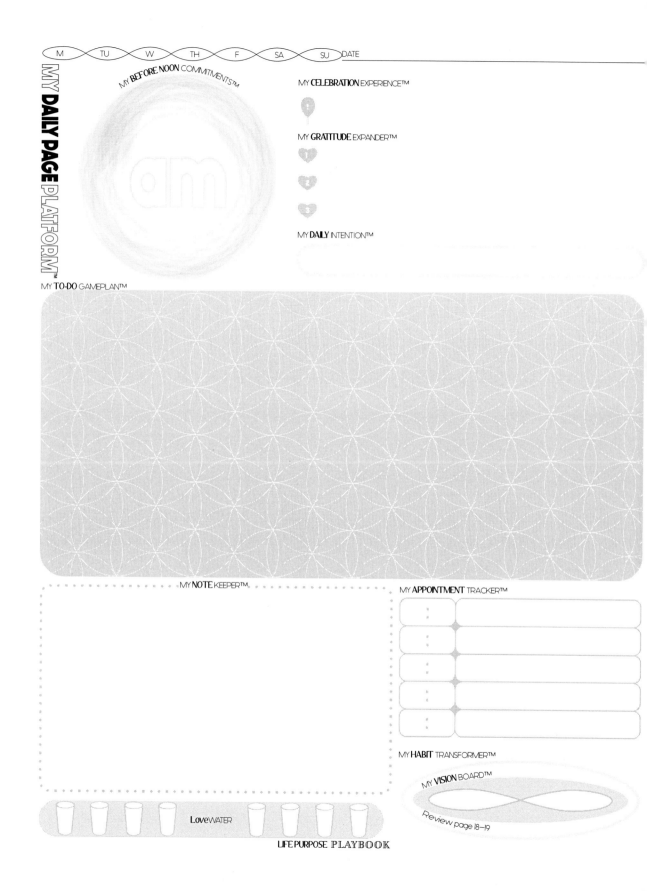

M   TU   W   TH   F   SA   SU   DATE

MY **DAILY PAGE** PLATFORM™

MY **BEFORE NOON** COMMITMENTS™

MY **CELEBRATION** EXPERIENCE™

MY **GRATITUDE** EXPANDER™

MY **DAILY** INTENTION™

MY **TO-DO** GAMEPLAN™

MY **NOTE** KEEPER™

MY **APPOINTMENT** TRACKER™

MY **HABIT** TRANSFORMER™

MY **VISION** BOARD™

Review page 18–19

Love WATER

LIFE PURPOSE PLAYBOOK

DATE _____ | M | TU | W | TH | F | SA | SU |

MY **CELEBRATION** EXPERIENCE™

MY **GRATITUDE** EXPANDER™

MY **DAILY** INTENTION™

MY **BEFORE NOON** COMMITMENTS™

MY DAILY PAGE PLATFORM™

MY **TO-DO** GAMEPLAN™

MY **APPOINTMENT** TRACKER™

MY **NOTE** KEEPER™

MY **HABIT** TRANSFORMER™

MY **VISION** BOARD™

Review page 18–19

Love WATER

LIFE PURPOSE PLAYBOOK

MY DAILY PAGE PLATFORM™

MY *BEFORE NOON* COMMITMENTS™

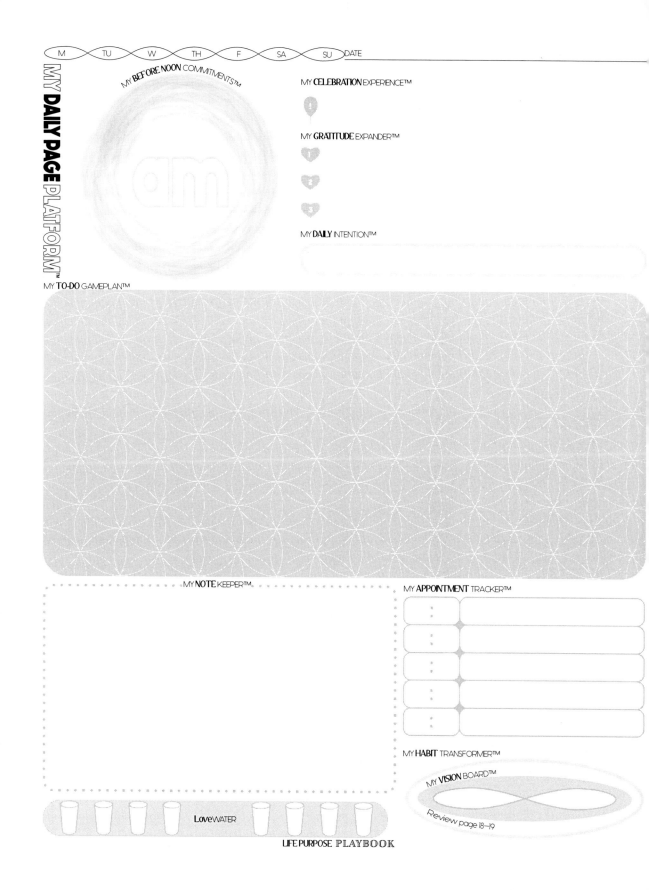

MY **CELEBRATION** EXPERIENCE™

MY **GRATITUDE** EXPANDER™

MY **DAILY** INTENTION™

MY **TO-DO** GAMEPLAN™

MY **NOTE** KEEPER™

MY **APPOINTMENT** TRACKER™

MY **HABIT** TRANSFORMER™

MY **VISION** BOARD™

Review page 18–19

Love WATER

LIFE PURPOSE PLAYBOOK

MY WEEKLY CELEBRATION EXPERIENCE™

MY OVERFLOW TASKS™

MY
LIFE VISION
REVIEW™

Add the dates to the next 7 pages of
MY DAILY PAGE PLATFORM™.

Now review the following sections of this playbook
& transfer any tasks or projects into those 7 pages.

Any that are not urgent for this week should be
scheduled into MY OVERFLOW TASKS
on the NEXT **WEEKLY CHECK-IN.**

MY LIFE INTENTION MATRIX™
(page 14)

MY CIRCLE OF LIFE EXPANDER™
(page 21)

MY GOAL CHARTING SYSTEM™
(page 24–25)

MY IDEA & PROJECT MAGNIFIER™
(page 26–27)

MY TO-DO CHECKLIST™
(page 28–29)

MY YEAR AHEAD OUTLOOK™
(page 31)

MY MONTHLY PLANNER™
(page 32–55)

MY 3 MUST-DO'S THIS WEEK™

MY **DAILY PAGE** PLATFORM™

M TU W TH F SA SU DATE

MY *BEFORE NOON* COMMITMENTS™

MY **CELEBRATION** EXPERIENCE™

MY **GRATITUDE** EXPANDER™

MY **DAILY** INTENTION™

MY **TO-DO** GAMEPLAN™

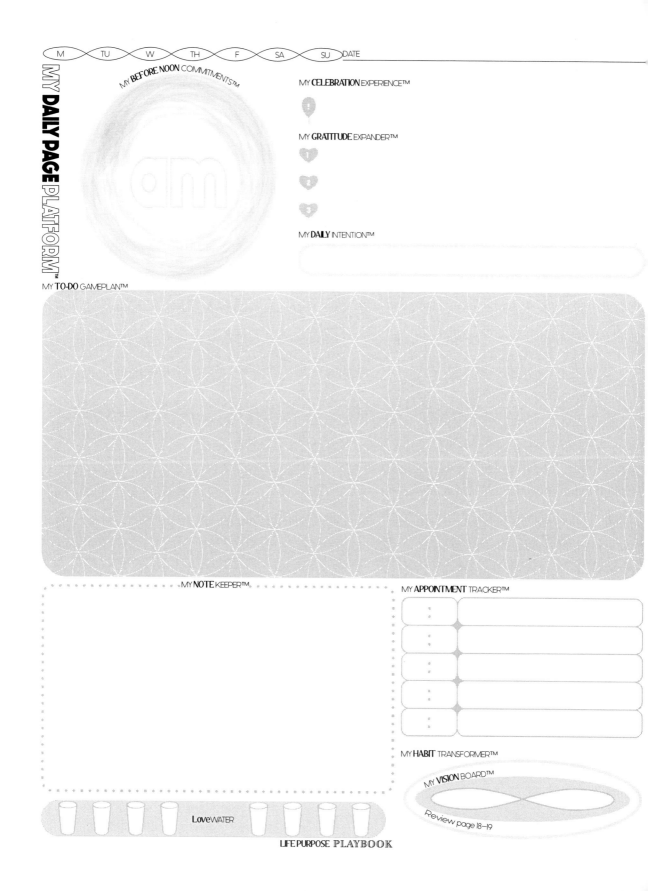

MY **NOTE** KEEPER™

MY **APPOINTMENT** TRACKER™

MY **HABIT** TRANSFORMER™

MY **VISION** BOARD™

Review page 18–19

Love WATER

LIFE PURPOSE PLAYBOOK

DATE _____

M | TU | W | TH | F | SA | SU

MY **CELEBRATION** EXPERIENCE™

MY **GRATITUDE** EXPANDER™

MY **DAILY** INTENTION™

MY **TO-DO** GAMEPLAN™

MY **BEFORE NOON** COMMITMENTS™

MY **DAILY PAGE** PLATFORM™

MY **APPOINTMENT** TRACKER™

MY **NOTE** KEEPER™

MY **HABIT** TRANSFORMER™

MY **VISION** BOARD™

Review page 18–19

Love WATER

LIFE PURPOSE PLAYBOOK

MY DAILY PAGE PLATFORM™

MY BEFORE NOON COMMITMENTS™

am

MY CELEBRATION EXPERIENCE™

MY GRATITUDE EXPANDER™

MY DAILY INTENTION™

MY TO-DO GAMEPLAN™

MY NOTE KEEPER™

MY APPOINTMENT TRACKER™

MY HABIT TRANSFORMER™

MY VISION BOARD™

Review page 18–19

Love WATER

LIFE PURPOSE PLAYBOOK

DATE _____

M TU W TH F SA SU

MY **CELEBRATION** EXPERIENCE™

MY **GRATITUDE** EXPANDER™

MY **DAILY** INTENTION™

MY **TO-DO** GAMEPLAN™

MY BEFORE **NOON** COMMITMENTS™

MY **DAILY PAGE** PLATFORM™

MY **APPOINTMENT** TRACKER™

MY **NOTE** KEEPER™

MY **HABIT** TRANSFORMER™

MY **VISION** BOARD™

Review page 18–19

LoveWATER

LIFE PURPOSE PLAYBOOK

MY DAILY PAGE PLATFORM™

MY **BEFORE NOON** COMMITMENTS™

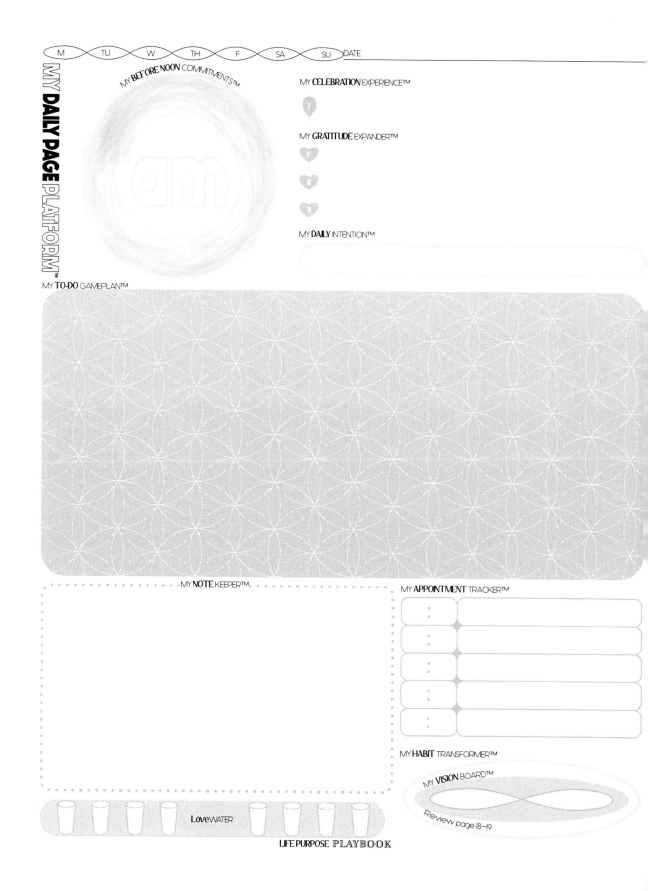

MY **CELEBRATION** EXPERIENCE™

MY **GRATITUDE** EXPANDER™

MY **DAILY** INTENTION™

MY **TO-DO** GAMEPLAN™

MY **NOTE** KEEPER™

MY **APPOINTMENT** TRACKER™

MY **HABIT** TRANSFORMER™

MY **VISION** BOARD™

Review page 18–19

Love WATER

LIFE PURPOSE PLAYBOOK

DATE _____

| M | TU | W | TH | F | SA | SU |

MY **CELEBRATION** EXPERIENCE™

MY **GRATITUDE** EXPANDER™

MY **DAILY** INTENTION™

MY BEFORE **NOON** COMMITMENTS™

MY DAILY PAGE PLATFORM™

MY **TO-DO** GAMEPLAN™

MY **APPOINTMENT** TRACKER™

MY **NOTE** KEEPER™

MY **HABIT** TRANSFORMER™

MY **VISION** BOARD™

Review page 18–19

Love WATER

LIFE PURPOSE PLAYBOOK

MY **DAILY PAGE** PLATFORM™

MY **BEFORE NOON** COMMITMENTS™

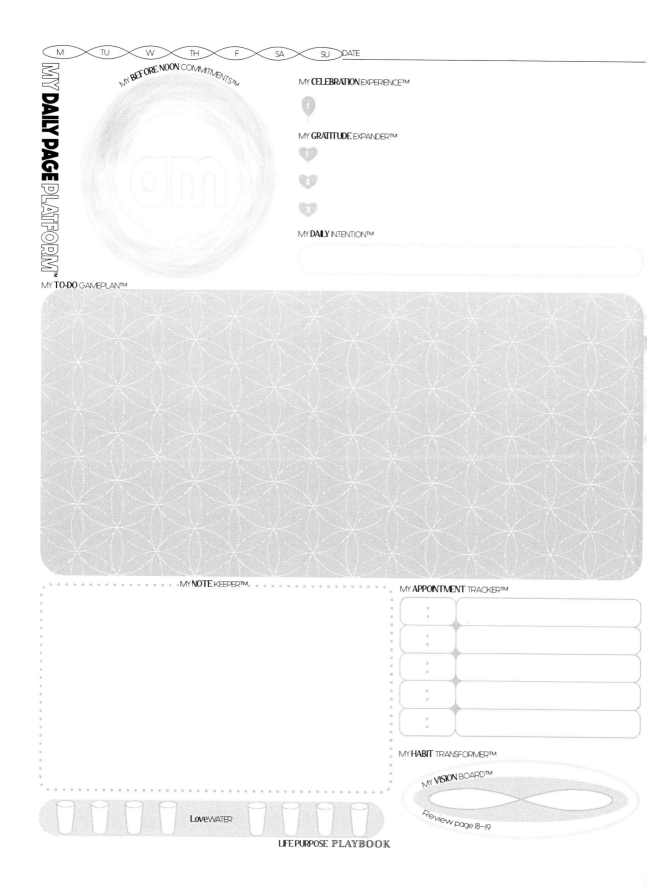

am

MY **CELEBRATION** EXPERIENCE™

MY **GRATITUDE** EXPANDER™

MY **DAILY** INTENTION™

MY **TO-DO** GAMEPLAN™

MY **NOTE** KEEPER™

MY **APPOINTMENT** TRACKER™

MY **HABIT** TRANSFORMER™

MY **VISION** BOARD™

Review page 18–19

Love WATER

LIFE PURPOSE PLAYBOOK

MY **WEEKLY** CELEBRATION EXPERIENCE™

MY
OVERFLOW
TASKS™

MY
LIFE VISION
REVIEW™

Add the dates to the next 7 pages of
MY DAILY PAGE PLATFORM™.

Now review the following sections of this playbook
& transfer any tasks or projects into those 7 pages.

Any that are not urgent for this week should be
scheduled into MY OVERFLOW TASKS
on the NEXT **WEEKLY CHECK-IN.**

MY LIFE INTENTION MATRIX™
(page 14)

MY CIRCLE OF LIFE EXPANDER™
(page 21)

MY GOAL CHARTING SYSTEM™
(page 24–25)

MY IDEA & PROJECT MAGNIFIER™
(page 26–27)

MY TO-DO CHECKLIST™
(page 28–29)

MY YEAR AHEAD OUTLOOK™
(page 31)

MY MONTHLY PLANNER™
(page 32–55)

MY **3 MUST-DO'S** THIS WEEK™

M   TU   W   TH   F   SA   SU   DATE _____

MY DAILY PAGE PLATFORM™

MY **BEFORE NOON** COMMITMENTS™

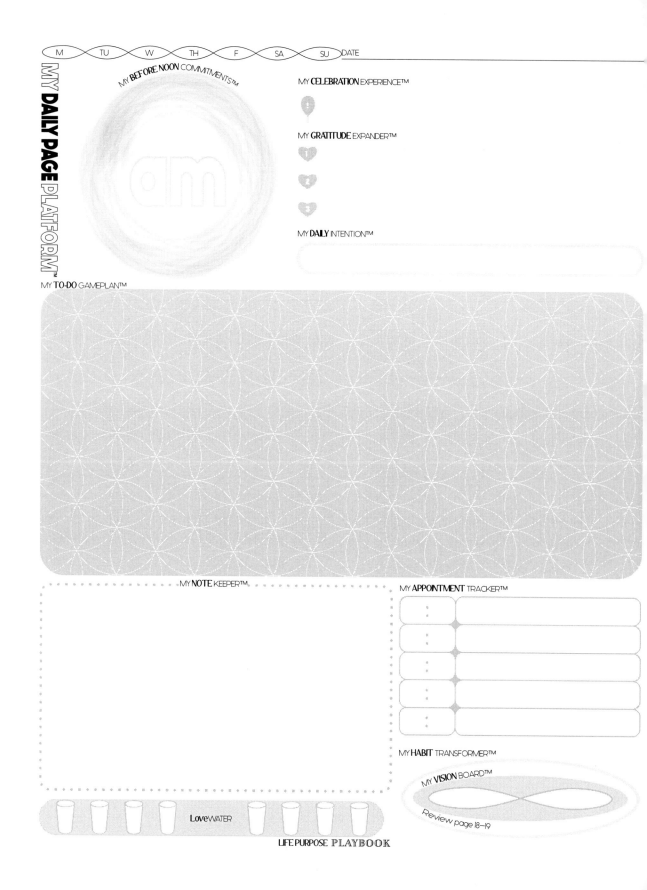

MY **CELEBRATION** EXPERIENCE™

MY **GRATITUDE** EXPANDER™

MY **DAILY** INTENTION™

MY **TO-DO** GAMEPLAN™

MY **NOTE** KEEPER™

MY **APPOINTMENT** TRACKER™

MY **HABIT** TRANSFORMER™

MY **VISION** BOARD™

Review page 18–19

Love WATER

LIFE PURPOSE **PLAYBOOK**

DATE _____

| M | TU | W | TH | F | SA | SU |

MY **CELEBRATION** EXPERIENCE™

MY **GRATITUDE** EXPANDER™

MY **DAILY** INTENTION™

MY **TO-DO** GAMEPLAN™

MY BEFORE **NOON** COMMITMENTS™

MY **DAILY PAGE** PLATFORM™

MY **APPOINTMENT** TRACKER™

MY **NOTE** KEEPER™

MY **HABIT** TRANSFORMER™

MY **VISION** BOARD™

Review page 18–19

Love WATER

LIFE PURPOSE PLAYBOOK

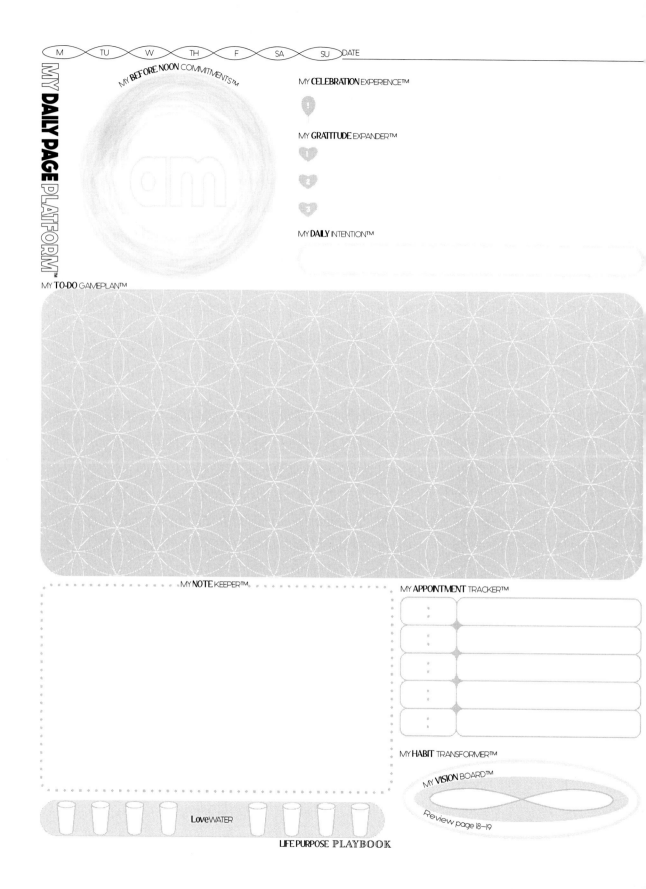

M TU W TH F SA SU DATE _____

MY DAILY PAGE PLATFORM™

MY BEFORE NOON COMMITMENTS™

MY CELEBRATION EXPERIENCE™

MY GRATITUDE EXPANDER™

MY DAILY INTENTION™

MY TO-DO GAMEPLAN™

MY NOTE KEEPER™

MY APPOINTMENT TRACKER™

MY HABIT TRANSFORMER™

MY VISION BOARD™

Review page 18–19

Love WATER

LIFE PURPOSE PLAYBOOK

DATE _____

| M | TU | W | TH | F | SA | SU |

MY **CELEBRATION** EXPERIENCE™

MY **GRATITUDE** EXPANDER™

MY **DAILY** INTENTION™

MY **TO-DO** GAMEPLAN™

MY BEFORE **NOON** COMMITMENTS™

MY **APPOINTMENT** TRACKER™

MY **NOTE** KEEPER™

MY **HABIT** TRANSFORMER™

MY **VISION** BOARD™

Review page 18–19

Love WATER

LIFE PURPOSE PLAYBOOK

M   TU   W   TH   F   SA   SU   DATE _____

MY **DAILY PAGE** PLATFORM™

MY **BEFORE NOON** COMMITMENTS™

am

MY **CELEBRATION** EXPERIENCE™

MY **GRATITUDE** EXPANDER™

1

2

3

MY **DAILY** INTENTION™

MY **TO-DO** GAMEPLAN™

MY **NOTE** KEEPER™

MY **APPOINTMENT** TRACKER™

MY **HABIT** TRANSFORMER™

MY **VISION** BOARD™

Review page 18–19

Love WATER

LIFE PURPOSE PLAYBOOK

DATE _____

| M | TU | W | TH | F | SA | SU |

MY **CELEBRATION** EXPERIENCE™

MY **GRATITUDE** EXPANDER™

MY **DAILY** INTENTION™

MY **TO-DO** GAMEPLAN™

MY BEFORE **NOON** COMMITMENTS™

MY **DAILY PAGE** PLATFORM™

MY **APPOINTMENT** TRACKER™

MY **NOTE** KEEPER™

MY **HABIT** TRANSFORMER™

MY **VISION** BOARD™

Review page 18–19

Love WATER

LIFE PURPOSE PLAYBOOK

M   TU   W   TH   F   SA   SU   DATE _____

MY **DAILY PAGE** PLATFORM™

MY **BEFORE NOON** COMMITMENTS™

MY **CELEBRATION** EXPERIENCE™

MY **GRATITUDE** EXPANDER™

MY **DAILY** INTENTION™

MY **TO-DO** GAMEPLAN™

MY **NOTE** KEEPER™

MY **APPOINTMENT** TRACKER™

MY **HABIT** TRANSFORMER™

MY **VISION** BOARD™

Review page 18—19

Love WATER

LIFE PURPOSE PLAYBOOK

MY WEEKLY CELEBRATION EXPERIENCE™

MY
OVERFLOW
TASKS™

MY
LIFE VISION
REVIEW™

Add the dates to the next 7 pages of
MY DAILY PAGE PLATFORM™.

Now review the following sections of this playbook
& transfer any tasks or projects into those 7 pages.

Any that are not urgent for this week should be
scheduled into MY OVERFLOW TASKS
on the NEXT **WEEKLY CHECK-IN.**

MY LIFE INTENTION MATRIX™
(page 14)

MY CIRCLE OF LIFE EXPANDER™
(page 21)

MY GOAL CHARTING SYSTEM™
(page 24–25)

MY IDEA & PROJECT MAGNIFIER™
(page 26–27)

MY TO-DO CHECKLIST™
(page 28–29)

MY YEAR AHEAD OUTLOOK™
(page 31)

MY MONTHLY PLANNER™
(page 32–55)

MY 3 MUST-DO'S THIS WEEK™

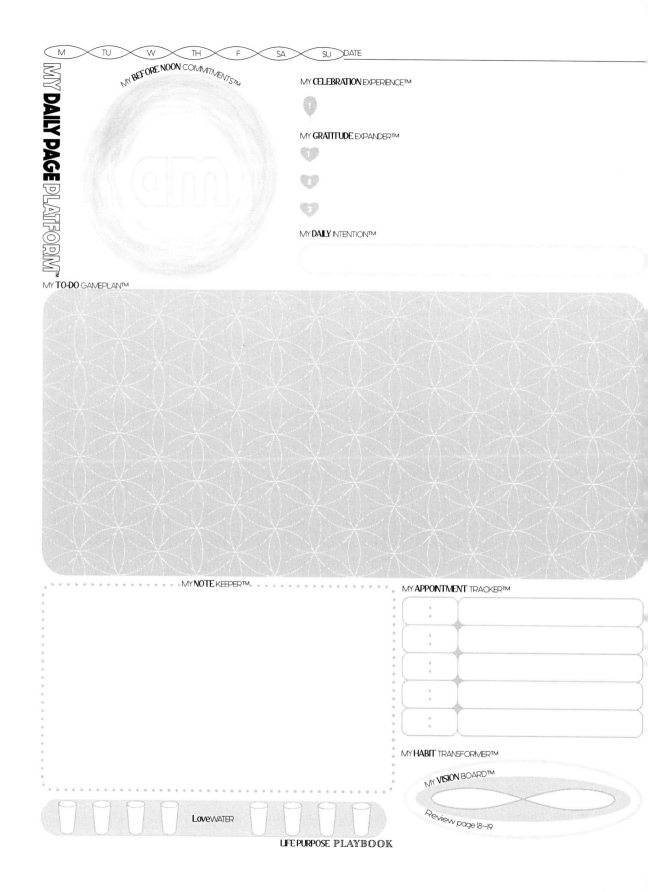

M   TU   W   TH   F   SA   SU   DATE _____

MY DAILY PAGE PLATFORM™

MY *BEFORE NOON* COMMITMENTS™

MY **CELEBRATION** EXPERIENCE™

MY **GRATITUDE** EXPANDER™

MY **DAILY** INTENTION™

MY **TO-DO** GAMEPLAN™

MY **NOTE** KEEPER™

MY **APPOINTMENT** TRACKER™

MY **HABIT** TRANSFORMER™

MY **VISION** BOARD™

Review page 18–19

Love WATER

LIFE PURPOSE PLAYBOOK

DATE _____

M TU W TH F SA SU

MY **CELEBRATION** EXPERIENCE™

MY **GRATITUDE** EXPANDER™

MY **DAILY** INTENTION™

MY BEFORE **NOON** COMMITMENTS™

MY **DAILY PAGE** PLATFORM™

MY **TO-DO** GAMEPLAN™

MY **APPOINTMENT** TRACKER™

MY **NOTE** KEEPER™

MY **HABIT** TRANSFORMER™

MY **VISION** BOARD™

Review page 18–19

Love WATER

LIFE PURPOSE PLAYBOOK

MY DAILY PAGE PLATFORM™

MY **BEFORE NOON** COMMITMENTS™

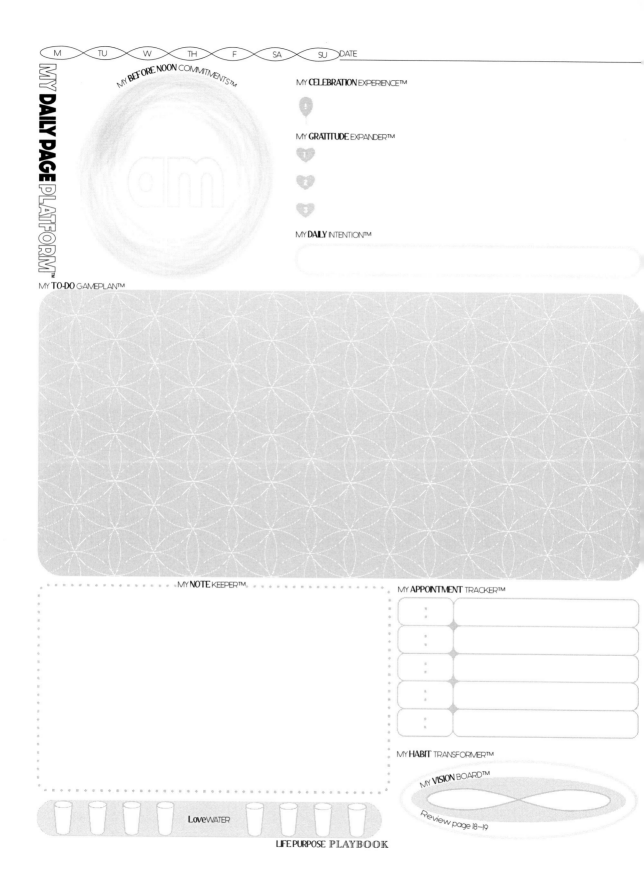

MY **CELEBRATION** EXPERIENCE™

MY **GRATITUDE** EXPANDER™

MY **DAILY** INTENTION™

MY **TO-DO** GAMEPLAN™

MY **NOTE** KEEPER™

MY **APPOINTMENT** TRACKER™

MY **HABIT** TRANSFORMER™

MY **VISION** BOARD™

Review page 18–19

Love WATER

LIFE PURPOSE PLAYBOOK

DATE _____ ⟨ M ⟩⟨ TU ⟩⟨ W ⟩⟨ TH ⟩⟨ F ⟩⟨ SA ⟩⟨ SU ⟩

MY **CELEBRATION** EXPERIENCE™

MY **GRATITUDE** EXPANDER™

MY **DAILY** INTENTION™

MY BEFORE **NOON** COMMITMENTS™

MY **DAILY PAGE** PLATFORM™

MY **TO-DO** GAMEPLAN™

MY **APPOINTMENT** TRACKER™

MY **NOTE** KEEPER™

MY **HABIT** TRANSFORMER™

MY **VISION** BOARD™

Review page 18–19

Love WATER

LIFE PURPOSE PLAYBOOK

MY DAILY PAGE PLATFORM™

MY *BEFORE NOON* COMMITMENTS™

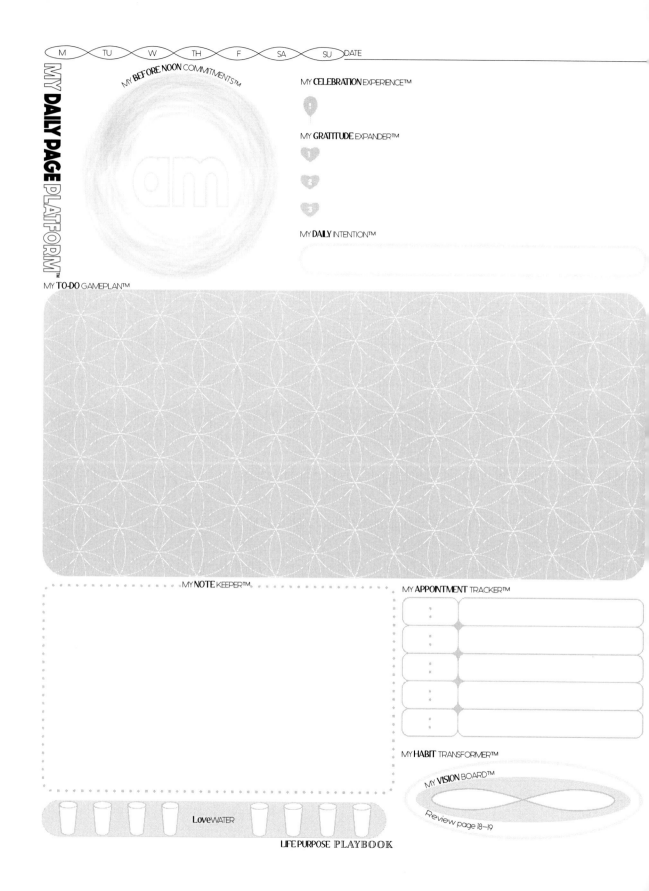

am

MY **CELEBRATION** EXPERIENCE™

MY **GRATITUDE** EXPANDER™

MY **DAILY** INTENTION™

MY **TO-DO** GAMEPLAN™

MY **NOTE** KEEPER™

MY **APPOINTMENT** TRACKER™

MY **HABIT** TRANSFORMER™

MY **VISION** BOARD™

Review page 18–19

Love WATER

LIFE PURPOSE PLAYBOOK

DATE _____ M TU W TH F SA SU

MY **CELEBRATION** EXPERIENCE™

MY **GRATITUDE** EXPANDER™

MY **DAILY** INTENTION™

MY **TO-DO** GAMEPLAN™

MY **APPOINTMENT** TRACKER™

MY **HABIT** TRANSFORMER™

MY **VISION** BOARD™

Review page 18–19

MY BEFORE **NOON** COMMITMENTS™

MY **DAILY PAGE** PLATFORM™

MY **NOTE** KEEPER™

Love WATER

LIFE PURPOSE PLAYBOOK

M | TU | W | TH | F | SA | SU | DATE

MY **DAILY PAGE** PLATFORM™

MY **BEFORE NOON** COMMITMENTS™

MY **CELEBRATION** EXPERIENCE™

MY **GRATITUDE** EXPANDER™

MY **DAILY** INTENTION™

MY **TO-DO** GAMEPLAN™

MY **NOTE** KEEPER™

MY **APPOINTMENT** TRACKER™

MY **HABIT** TRANSFORMER™

MY **VISION** BOARD™

Review page 18—19

Love WATER

LIFE PURPOSE PLAYBOOK

MY **WEEKLY** CELEBRATION EXPERIENCE™

MY OVERFLOW TASKS™

MY
LIFE VISION
REVIEW™

Add the dates to the next 7 pages of
MY DAILY PAGE PLATFORM™.

Now review the following sections of this playbook
& transfer any tasks or projects into those 7 pages.

Any that are not urgent for this week should be
scheduled into MY OVERFLOW TASKS
on the NEXT **WEEKLY CHECK-IN.**

MY LIFE INTENTION MATRIX™
(page 14)

MY CIRCLE OF LIFE EXPANDER™
(page 21)

MY GOAL CHARTING SYSTEM™
(page 24—25)

MY IDEA & PROJECT MAGNIFIER™
(page 26—27)

MY TO-DO CHECKLIST™
(page 28—29)

MY YEAR AHEAD OUTLOOK™
(page 31)

MY MONTHLY PLANNER™
(page 32—55)

MY **3 MUST-DO's** THIS WEEK™

MY DAILY PAGE PLATFORM™

M | TU | W | TH | F | SA | SU | DATE _____

MY BEFORE NOON COMMITMENTS™

MY CELEBRATION EXPERIENCE™

MY GRATITUDE EXPANDER™

MY DAILY INTENTION™

MY TO-DO GAMEPLAN™

MY NOTE KEEPER™

MY APPOINTMENT TRACKER™

MY HABIT TRANSFORMER™

MY VISION BOARD™

Review page 18–19

Love WATER

LIFE PURPOSE PLAYBOOK

DATE _____

M | TU | W | TH | F | SA | SU

MY **CELEBRATION** EXPERIENCE™

MY **GRATITUDE** EXPANDER™

MY **DAILY** INTENTION™

MY **BEFORE NOON** COMMITMENTS™

MY **DAILY PAGE** PLATFORM™

MY **TO-DO** GAMEPLAN™

MY **APPOINTMENT** TRACKER™

MY **NOTE** KEEPER™

MY **HABIT** TRANSFORMER™

MY **VISION** BOARD™

Review page 18–19

Love WATER

LIFE PURPOSE PLAYBOOK

M TU W TH F SA SU DATE _____

MY **DAILY PAGE** PLATFORM™

MY **BEFORE NOON** COMMITMENTS™

am

MY **CELEBRATION** EXPERIENCE™

MY **GRATITUDE** EXPANDER™

MY **DAILY** INTENTION™

MY **TO-DO** GAMEPLAN™

.... MY **NOTE** KEEPER™ ....

MY **APPOINTMENT** TRACKER™

MY **HABIT** TRANSFORMER™

MY **VISION** BOARD™

Review page 18–19

Love WATER

LIFE PURPOSE PLAYBOOK

DATE _____

| M | TU | W | TH | F | SA | SU |

MY **CELEBRATION** EXPERIENCE™

MY **GRATITUDE** EXPANDER™

MY **DAILY** INTENTION™

MY **TO-DO** GAMEPLAN™

MY BEFORE **NOON** COMMITMENTS™

MY **DAILY PAGE** PLATFORM™

MY **APPOINTMENT** TRACKER™

※ MY **NOTE** KEEPER™ ※

MY **HABIT** TRANSFORMER™

MY **VISION** BOARD™

Review page 18–19

Love WATER

LIFE PURPOSE PLAYBOOK

M | TU | W | TH | F | SA | SU | DATE _____

MY DAILY PAGE PLATFORM™

MY *BEFORE NOON* COMMITMENTS™

am

MY **CELEBRATION** EXPERIENCE™

MY **GRATITUDE** EXPANDER™

MY **DAILY** INTENTION™

MY **TO-DO** GAMEPLAN™

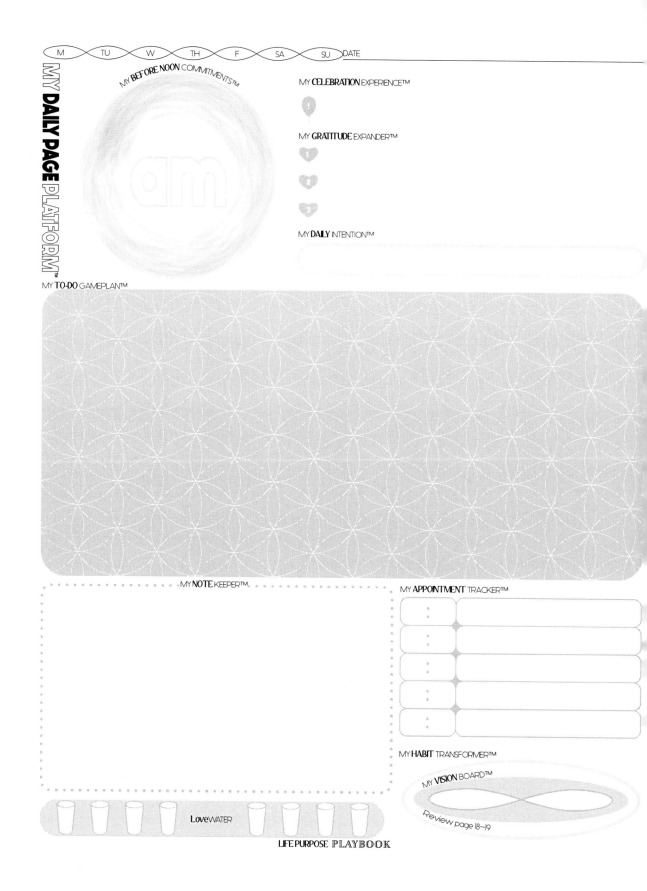

MY **NOTE** KEEPER™

MY **APPOINTMENT** TRACKER™

MY **HABIT** TRANSFORMER™

MY **VISION** BOARD™

Review page 18–19

Love WATER

LIFE PURPOSE PLAYBOOK

DATE _____

MY **CELEBRATION** EXPERIENCE™

MY **GRATITUDE** EXPANDER™

MY **DAILY** INTENTION™

MY BEFORE **NOON** COMMITMENTS™

MY **DAILY PAGE** PLATFORM™

MY **TO-DO** GAMEPLAN™

MY **APPOINTMENT** TRACKER™

MY **NOTE** KEEPER™

MY **HABIT** TRANSFORMER™

MY **VISION** BOARD™

Review page 18–19

LoveWATER

LIFE PURPOSE PLAYBOOK

MY **DAILY PAGE** PLATFORM™

MY *BEFORE NOON* COMMITMENTS™

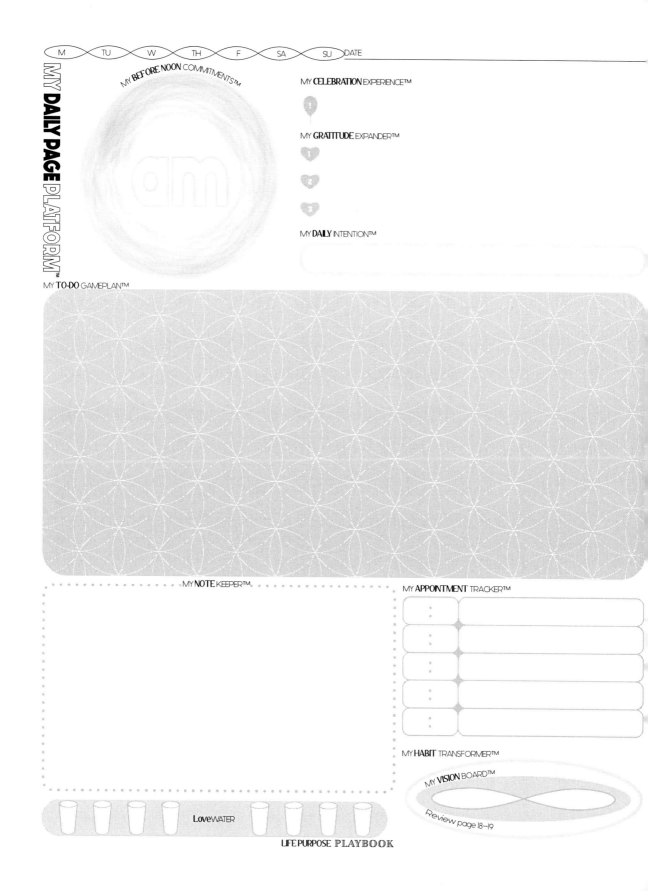

MY **CELEBRATION** EXPERIENCE™

MY **GRATITUDE** EXPANDER™

MY **DAILY** INTENTION™

MY **TO-DO** GAMEPLAN™

MY **NOTE** KEEPER™

MY **APPOINTMENT** TRACKER™

MY **HABIT** TRANSFORMER™

MY **VISION** BOARD™

Review page 18–19

Love WATER

LIFE PURPOSE PLAYBOOK

MY **WEEKLY** CELEBRATION EXPERIENCE™

MY
OVERFLOW
TASKS™

MY
LIFE VISION
REVIEW™

Add the dates to the next 7 pages of
MY DAILY PAGE PLATFORM™.

. . . .

Now review the following sections of this playbook
& transfer any tasks or projects into those 7 pages.

Any that are not urgent for this week should be
scheduled into MY OVERFLOW TASKS
on the NEXT **WEEKLY CHECK-IN.**

MY LIFE INTENTION MATRIX™
(page 14) ⭘

MY CIRCLE OF LIFE EXPANDER™
(page 21) ⭘

MY GOAL CHARTING SYSTEM™
(page 24–25) ⭘

MY IDEA & PROJECT MAGNIFIER™
(page 26–27) ⭘

MY TO–DO CHECKLIST™
(page 28–29) ⭘

MY YEAR AHEAD OUTLOOK™
(page 31) ⭘

MY MONTHLY PLANNER™
(page 32–55) ⭘

MY **3 MUST-DO**'S THIS WEEK™

M TU W TH F SA SU DATE _____

MY *DAILY PAGE* PLATFORM™

MY *BEFORE NOON* COMMITMENTS™

am

MY *CELEBRATION* EXPERIENCE™

MY *GRATITUDE* EXPANDER™

MY *DAILY* INTENTION™

MY *TO-DO* GAMEPLAN™

MY *NOTE* KEEPER™

MY *APPOINTMENT* TRACKER™

MY *HABIT* TRANSFORMER™

MY *VISION* BOARD™

Review page 18–19

Love WATER

LIFE PURPOSE PLAYBOOK

DATE _____ | M | TU | W | TH | F | SA | SU |

MY **CELEBRATION** EXPERIENCE™

MY **GRATITUDE** EXPANDER™

MY **DAILY** INTENTION™

MY **BEFORE NOON** COMMITMENTS™

MY **DAILY PAGE** PLATFORM™

MY **TO-DO** GAMEPLAN™

MY **APPOINTMENT** TRACKER™

MY **NOTE** KEEPER™

MY **HABIT** TRANSFORMER™

MY **VISION** BOARD™

Review page 18–19

Love WATER

LIFE PURPOSE PLAYBOOK

MY **DAILY PAGE** PLATFORM™

MY **BEFORE NOON** COMMITMENTS™

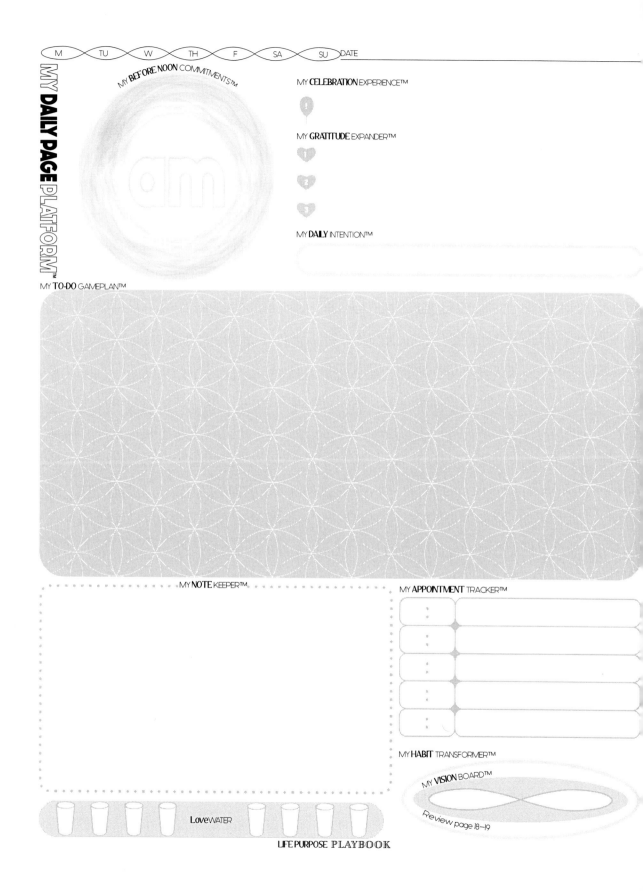

MY **CELEBRATION** EXPERIENCE™

MY **GRATITUDE** EXPANDER™

MY **DAILY** INTENTION™

MY **TO-DO** GAMEPLAN™

MY **NOTE** KEEPER™

MY **APPOINTMENT** TRACKER™

MY **HABIT** TRANSFORMER™

MY **VISION** BOARD™

Review page 18–19

Love WATER

LIFE PURPOSE PLAYBOOK

DATE _____

| M | TU | W | TH | F | SA | SU |

MY **CELEBRATION** EXPERIENCE™

MY **GRATITUDE** EXPANDER™

MY **DAILY** INTENTION™

MY BEFORE **NOON** COMMITMENTS™

MY **TO-DO** GAMEPLAN™

MY **APPOINTMENT** TRACKER™

MY **NOTE** KEEPER™

MY **HABIT** TRANSFORMER™

MY **VISION** BOARD™

Review page 18–19

Love WATER

LIFE PURPOSE PLAYBOOK

MY **DAILY PAGE** PLATFORM™

MY *BEFORE NOON* COMMITMENTS™

am

MY **CELEBRATION** EXPERIENCE™

MY **GRATITUDE** EXPANDER™

MY **DAILY** INTENTION™

MY **TO-DO** GAMEPLAN™

····· MY **NOTE** KEEPER™ ·····

MY **APPOINTMENT** TRACKER™

MY **HABIT** TRANSFORMER™

MY **VISION** BOARD™

Review page 18–19

Love WATER

LIFE PURPOSE PLAYBOOK

DATE _____ | M | TU | W | TH | F | SA | SU |

MY **CELEBRATION** EXPERIENCE™

MY **GRATITUDE** EXPANDER™

MY **DAILY** INTENTION™

MY **TO-DO** GAMEPLAN™

MY **APPOINTMENT** TRACKER™

MY **NOTE** KEEPER™

MY **HABIT** TRANSFORMER™

MY **VISION** BOARD™

Review page 18–19

Love WATER

LIFE PURPOSE PLAYBOOK

MY DAILY PAGE PLATFORM™

MY *BEFORE NOON* COMMITMENTS™

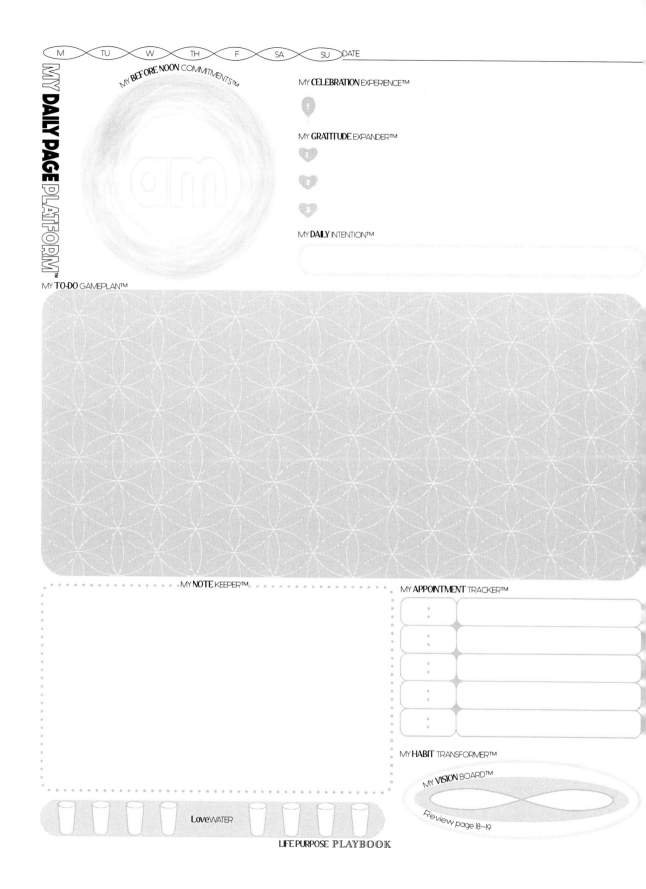

MY *CELEBRATION* EXPERIENCE™

MY *GRATITUDE* EXPANDER™

MY *DAILY* INTENTION™

MY *TO-DO* GAMEPLAN™

MY *NOTE* KEEPER™

MY *APPOINTMENT* TRACKER™

MY *HABIT* TRANSFORMER™

MY *VISION* BOARD™

Review page 18—19

Love WATER

LIFE PURPOSE PLAYBOOK

MY WEEKLY CELEBRATION EXPERIENCE™

MY
OVERFLOW
TASKS™

MY
LIFE VISION
REVIEW™

Add the dates to the next 7 pages of
MY DAILY PAGE PLATFORM™.

Now review the following sections of this playbook
& transfer any tasks or projects into those 7 pages.

Any that are not urgent for this week should be
scheduled into MY OVERFLOW TASKS
on the NEXT **WEEKLY CHECK-IN.**

MY LIFE INTENTION MATRIX™
(page 14)

MY CIRCLE OF LIFE EXPANDER™
(page 21)

MY GOAL CHARTING SYSTEM™
(page 24–25)

MY IDEA & PROJECT MAGNIFIER™
(page 26–27)

MY TO–DO CHECKLIST™
(page 28–29)

MY YEAR AHEAD OUTLOOK™
(page 31)

MY MONTHLY PLANNER™
(page 32–55)

MY 3 MUST-DO'S THIS WEEK™

M | TU | W | TH | F | SA | SU | DATE _____

MY **DAILY PAGE** PLATFORM™

MY **BEFORE NOON** COMMITMENTS™

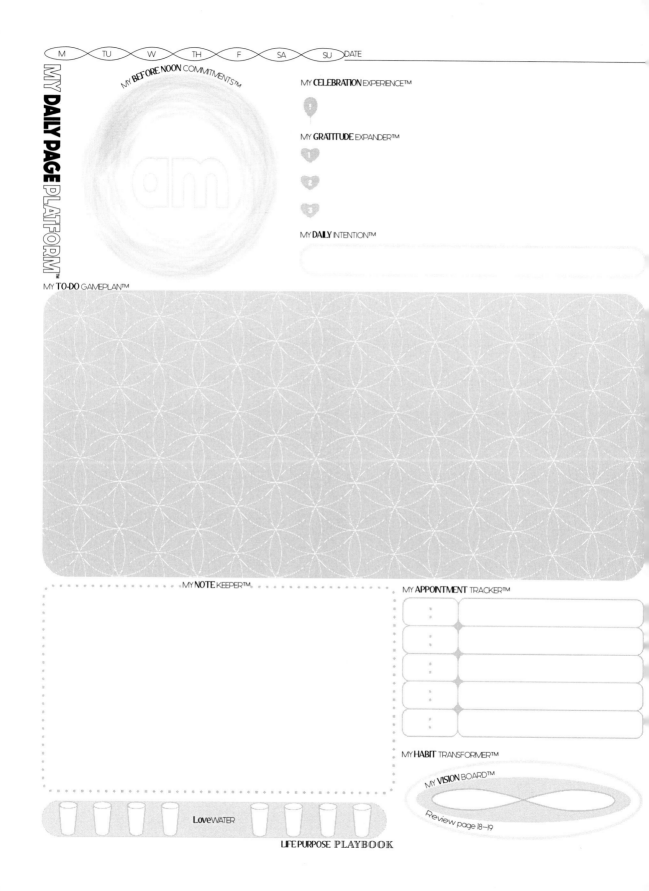

am

MY **CELEBRATION** EXPERIENCE™

MY **GRATITUDE** EXPANDER™

MY **DAILY** INTENTION™

MY **TO-DO** GAMEPLAN™

MY **NOTE** KEEPER™

MY **APPOINTMENT** TRACKER™

MY **HABIT** TRANSFORMER™

MY **VISION** BOARD™

Review page 18–19

Love WATER

LIFE PURPOSE PLAYBOOK

DATE _____

| M | TU | W | TH | F | SA | SU |

MY **CELEBRATION** EXPERIENCE™

MY **GRATITUDE** EXPANDER™

MY **DAILY** INTENTION™

MY BEFORE **NOON** COMMITMENTS™

MY **TO-DO** GAMEPLAN™

MY **APPOINTMENT** TRACKER™

MY **NOTE** KEEPER™

MY **HABIT** TRANSFORMER™

MY **VISION** BOARD™

Review page 18–19

Love WATER

LIFE PURPOSE PLAYBOOK

MY **DAILY PAGE** PLATFORM™

MY *BEFORE NOON* COMMITMENTS™

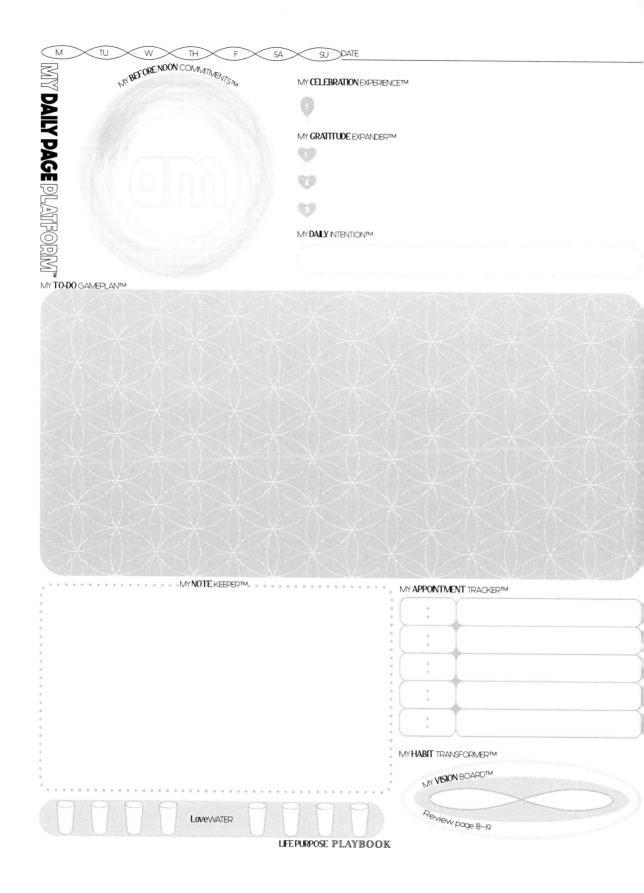

am

MY **CELEBRATION** EXPERIENCE™

MY **GRATITUDE** EXPANDER™

MY **DAILY** INTENTION™

MY **TO-DO** GAMEPLAN™

MY **NOTE** KEEPER™

MY **APPOINTMENT** TRACKER™

MY **HABIT** TRANSFORMER™

MY **VISION** BOARD™

Review page 18–19

Love WATER

LIFE PURPOSE PLAYBOOK

DATE _____ | M | TU | W | TH | F | SA | SU |

MY **CELEBRATION** EXPERIENCE™

MY **GRATITUDE** EXPANDER™

MY **DAILY** INTENTION™

MY **TO-DO** GAMEPLAN™

MY BEFORE **NOON** COMMITMENTS™

MY **DAILY PAGE** PLATFORM™

MY **APPOINTMENT** TRACKER™

MY **NOTE** KEEPER™

MY **HABIT** TRANSFORMER™

MY **VISION** BOARD™

Review page 18–19

Love WATER

LIFE PURPOSE PLAYBOOK

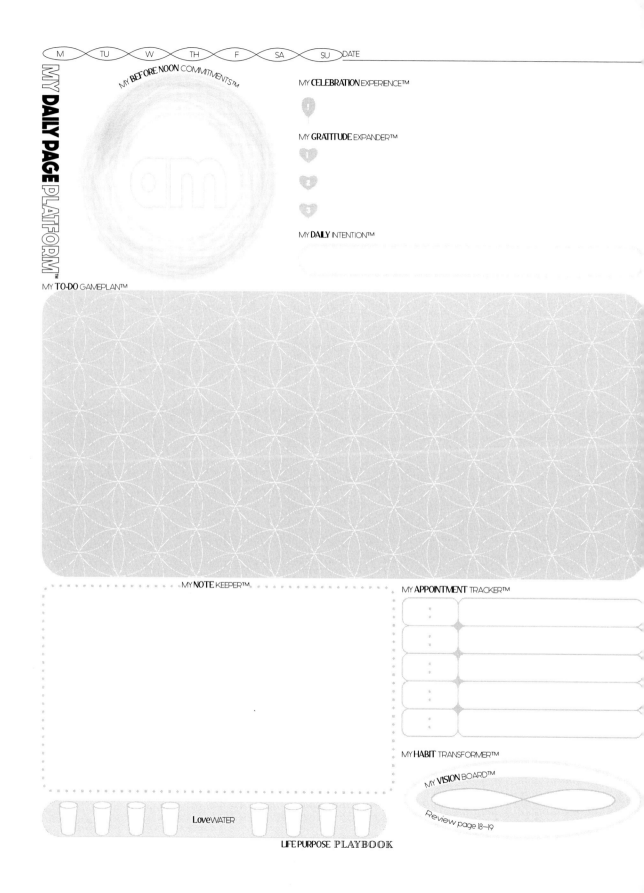

M | TU | W | TH | F | SA | SU | DATE

MY DAILY PAGE PLATFORM™

MY BEFORE NOON COMMITMENTS™

MY CELEBRATION EXPERIENCE™

MY GRATITUDE EXPANDER™

MY DAILY INTENTION™

MY TO-DO GAMEPLAN™

MY NOTE KEEPER™

MY APPOINTMENT TRACKER™

MY HABIT TRANSFORMER™

MY VISION BOARD™

Review page 18–19

Love WATER

LIFE PURPOSE PLAYBOOK

DATE _____ | M | TU | W | TH | F | SA | SU |

MY **CELEBRATION** EXPERIENCE™

MY **GRATITUDE** EXPANDER™

MY **DAILY** INTENTION™

MY **TO-DO** GAMEPLAN™

MY BEFORE **NOON** COMMITMENTS™

MY **DAILY PAGE** PLATFORM™

MY **APPOINTMENT** TRACKER™

MY **NOTE** KEEPER™

MY **HABIT** TRANSFORMER™

MY **VISION** BOARD™

Review page 18–19

Love WATER

LIFE PURPOSE PLAYBOOK

MY **DAILY PAGE** PLATFORM™

MY **BEFORE NOON** COMMITMENTS™

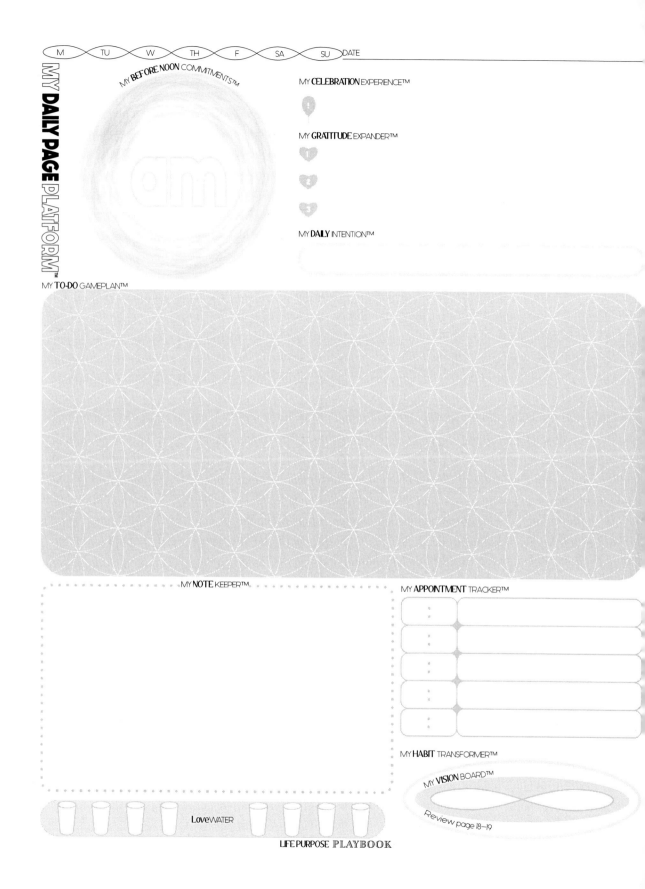

MY **CELEBRATION** EXPERIENCE™

MY **GRATITUDE** EXPANDER™

MY **DAILY** INTENTION™

MY **TO-DO** GAMEPLAN™

MY **NOTE** KEEPER™

MY **APPOINTMENT** TRACKER™

MY **HABIT** TRANSFORMER™

MY **VISION** BOARD™

Review page 18—19

Love WATER

LIFE PURPOSE PLAYBOOK

MY WEEKLY CELEBRATION EXPERIENCE™

MY
OVERFLOW
TASKS™

MY
LIFE VISION
REVIEW™

Add the dates to the next 7 pages of
MY DAILY PAGE PLATFORM™.

Now review the following sections of this playbook
& transfer any tasks or projects into those 7 pages.

Any that are not urgent for this week should be
scheduled into MY OVERFLOW TASKS
on the NEXT **WEEKLY CHECK-IN.**

MY LIFE INTENTION MATRIX™
(page 14) ○

MY CIRCLE OF LIFE EXPANDER™
(page 21) ○

MY GOAL CHARTING SYSTEM™
(page 24—25) ○

MY IDEA & PROJECT MAGNIFIER™
(page 26—27) ○

MY TO-DO CHECKLIST™
(page 28—29) ○

MY YEAR AHEAD OUTLOOK™
(page 31) ○

MY MONTHLY PLANNER™
(page 32—55) ○

MY **3 MUST-DO'S** THIS WEEK™

MY **DAILY PAGE** PLATFORM™

MY *BEFORE NOON* COMMITMENTS™

am

MY **CELEBRATION** EXPERIENCE™

MY **GRATITUDE** EXPANDER™

1

2

3

MY **DAILY** INTENTION™

MY **TO-DO** GAMEPLAN™

MY **NOTE** KEEPER™

MY **APPOINTMENT** TRACKER™

MY **HABIT** TRANSFORMER™

MY **VISION** BOARD™

Review page 18–19

Love WATER

LIFE PURPOSE PLAYBOOK

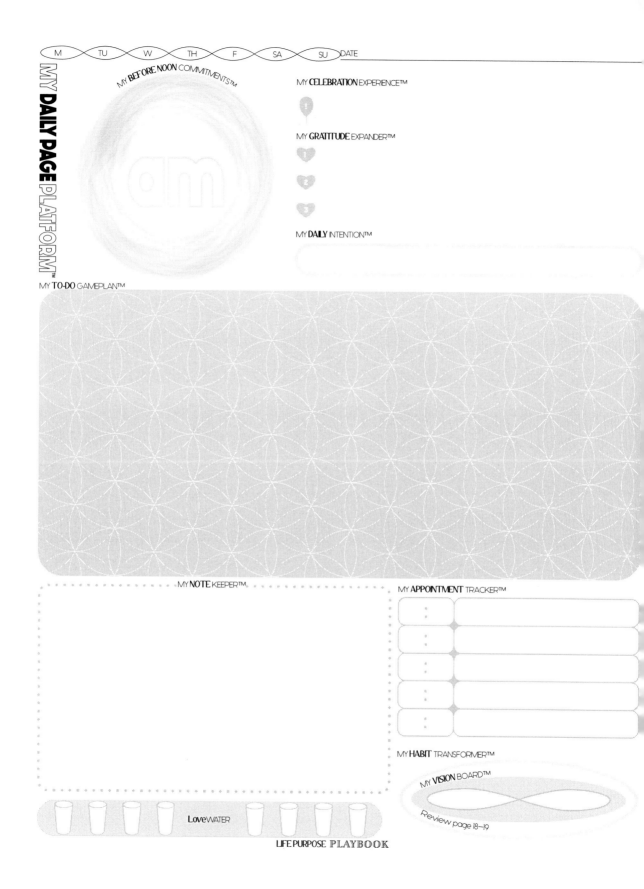

DATE _____ ⟨ M ⟩⟨ TU ⟩⟨ W ⟩⟨ TH ⟩⟨ F ⟩⟨ SA ⟩⟨ SU ⟩

MY **CELEBRATION** EXPERIENCE™

MY **GRATITUDE** EXPANDER™

MY **DAILY** INTENTION™

MY BEFORE **NOON** COMMITMENTS™

MY **DAILY PAGE** PLATFORM™

MY **TO-DO** GAMEPLAN™

MY **APPOINTMENT** TRACKER™

MY **NOTE** KEEPER™

MY **HABIT** TRANSFORMER™

MY **VISION** BOARD™

Review page 18–19

Love WATER

LIFE PURPOSE PLAYBOOK

MY **DAILY** PAGE PLATFORM™

MY *BEFORE NOON* COMMITMENTS™

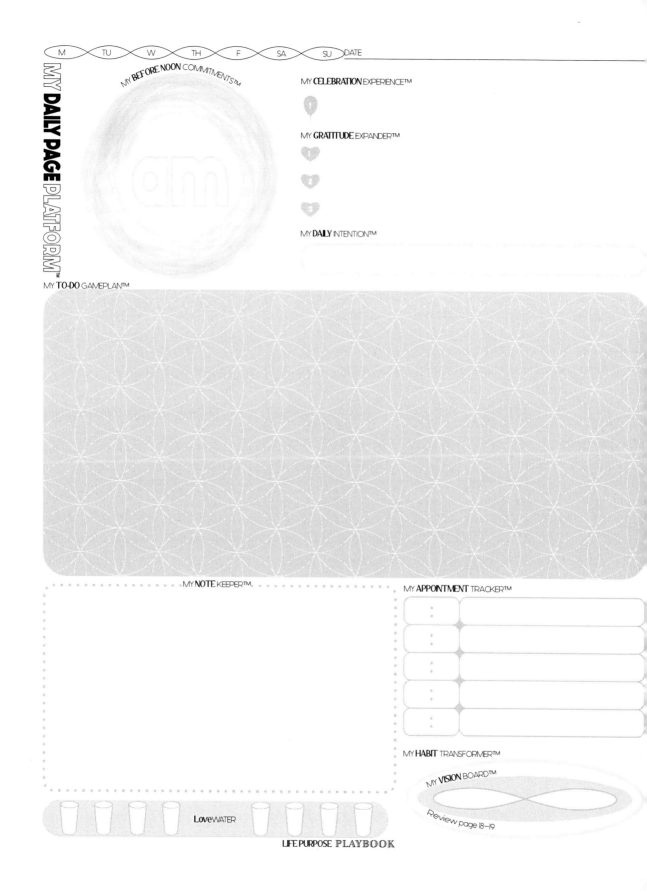

am

MY **CELEBRATION** EXPERIENCE™

MY **GRATITUDE** EXPANDER™

MY **DAILY** INTENTION™

MY **TO-DO** GAMEPLAN™

MY **NOTE** KEEPER™

MY **APPOINTMENT** TRACKER™

MY **HABIT** TRANSFORMER™

MY **VISION** BOARD™

Review page 18–19

Love WATER

LIFE PURPOSE PLAYBOOK

DATE _____

| M | TU | W | TH | F | SA | SU |

MY **CELEBRATION** EXPERIENCE™

MY **GRATITUDE** EXPANDER™

MY **DAILY** INTENTION™

MY **TO-DO** GAMEPLAN™

MY BEFORE **NOON** COMMITMENTS™

MY **DAILY PAGE** PLATFORM™

MY **APPOINTMENT** TRACKER™

MY **NOTE** KEEPER™

MY **HABIT** TRANSFORMER™

MY **VISION** BOARD™

Review page 18–19

Love WATER

LIFE PURPOSE PLAYBOOK

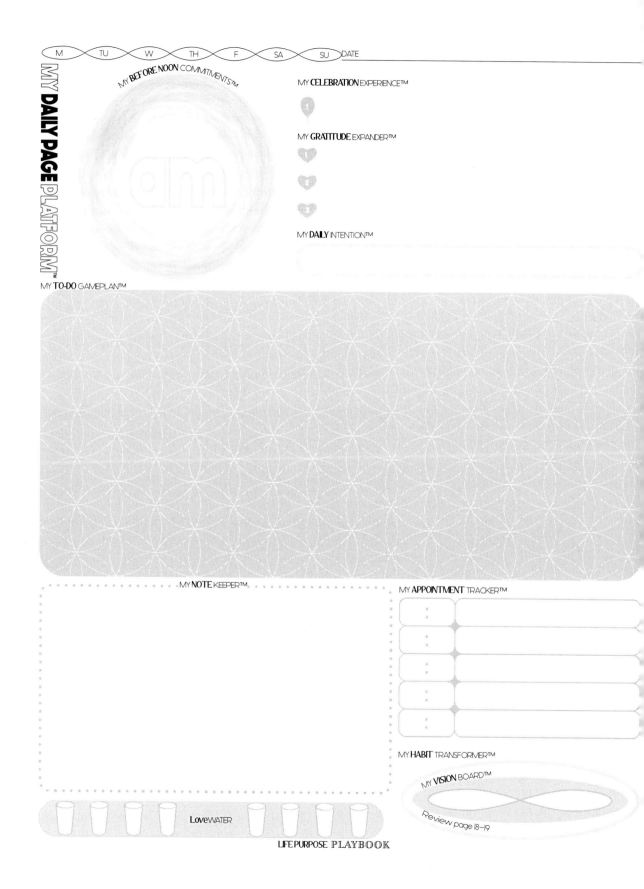

M   TU   W   TH   F   SA   SU   DATE _____

MY **DAILY PAGE** PLATFORM™

MY **BEFORE NOON** COMMITMENTS™

MY **CELEBRATION** EXPERIENCE™

MY **GRATITUDE** EXPANDER™

MY **DAILY** INTENTION™

MY **TO-DO** GAMEPLAN™

MY **NOTE** KEEPER™

MY **APPOINTMENT** TRACKER™

MY **HABIT** TRANSFORMER™

MY **VISION** BOARD™

Review page 18–19

Love WATER

LIFE PURPOSE PLAYBOOK

DATE _____

| M | TU | W | TH | F | SA | SU |

MY **CELEBRATION** EXPERIENCE™

MY **GRATITUDE** EXPANDER™

MY **DAILY** INTENTION™

MY **TO-DO** GAMEPLAN™

MY BEFORE **NOON** COMMITMENTS™

MY DAILY PAGE PLATFORM™

MY **APPOINTMENT** TRACKER™

MY **NOTE** KEEPER™

MY **HABIT** TRANSFORMER™

MY **VISION** BOARD™

Review page 18—19

LoveWATER

LIFE PURPOSE PLAYBOOK

M | TU | W | TH | F | SA | SU | DATE _____

MY DAILY PAGE PLATFORM™

MY BEFORE NOON COMMITMENTS™

MY CELEBRATION EXPERIENCE™

MY GRATITUDE EXPANDER™

MY DAILY INTENTION™

MY TO-DO GAMEPLAN™

MY NOTE KEEPER™

MY APPOINTMENT TRACKER™

MY HABIT TRANSFORMER™

MY VISION BOARD™

Review page 18–19

Love WATER

LIFE PURPOSE PLAYBOOK

MY WEEKLY CELEBRATION EXPERIENCE™

MY OVERFLOW TASKS™

MY
LIFE VISION
REVIEW™

Add the dates to the next 7 pages of
MY DAILY PAGE PLATFORM™.

Now review the following sections of this playbook
& transfer any tasks or projects into those 7 pages.

Any that are not urgent for this week should be
scheduled into MY OVERFLOW TASKS
on the NEXT **WEEKLY CHECK-IN.**

MY LIFE INTENTION MATRIX™
(page 14)

MY CIRCLE OF LIFE EXPANDER™
(page 21)

MY GOAL CHARTING SYSTEM™
(page 24–25)

MY IDEA & PROJECT MAGNIFIER™
(page 26–27)

MY TO-DO CHECKLIST™
(page 28–29)

MY YEAR AHEAD OUTLOOK™
(page 31)

MY MONTHLY PLANNER™
(page 32–55)

MY 3 MUST-DO's THIS WEEK™

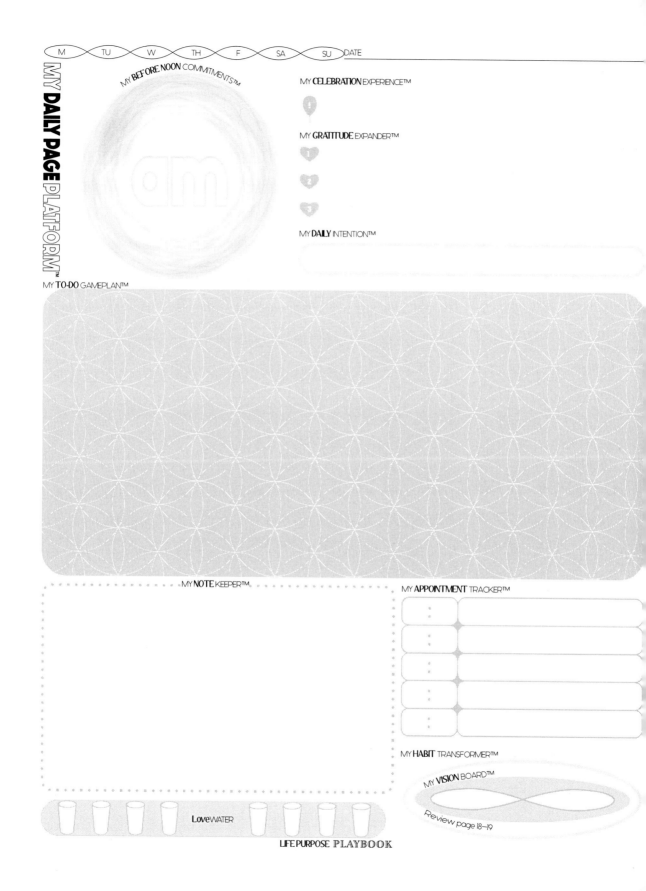

M | TU | W | TH | F | SA | SU | DATE _____

MY **DAILY PAGE** PLATFORM™

MY BEFORE NOON COMMITMENTS™

MY **CELEBRATION** EXPERIENCE™

MY **GRATITUDE** EXPANDER™

MY **DAILY** INTENTION™

MY **TO-DO** GAMEPLAN™

MY **NOTE** KEEPER™

MY **APPOINTMENT** TRACKER™

MY **HABIT** TRANSFORMER™

MY **VISION** BOARD™

Review page 18–19

Love WATER

LIFE PURPOSE PLAYBOOK

DATE _____

MY **CELEBRATION** EXPERIENCE™

MY **GRATITUDE** EXPANDER™

MY **DAILY** INTENTION™

MY BEFORE **NOON** COMMITMENTS™

MY **TO-DO** GAMEPLAN™

MY **APPOINTMENT** TRACKER™

MY **NOTE** KEEPER™

MY **HABIT** TRANSFORMER™

MY **VISION** BOARD™

Review page 18–19

Love WATER

LIFE PURPOSE PLAYBOOK

MY **DAILY PAGE** PLATFORM™

MY **BEFORE NOON** COMMITMENTS™

MY **CELEBRATION** EXPERIENCE™

MY **GRATITUDE** EXPANDER™

MY **DAILY** INTENTION™

MY **TO-DO** GAMEPLAN™

MY **NOTE** KEEPER™

MY **APPOINTMENT** TRACKER™

MY **HABIT** TRANSFORMER™

MY **VISION** BOARD™

Review page 18—19

Love WATER

LIFE PURPOSE PLAYBOOK

DATE | M | TU | W | TH | F | SA | SU

MY **CELEBRATION** EXPERIENCE™

MY **GRATITUDE** EXPANDER™

MY **DAILY** INTENTION™

MY **TO-DO** GAMEPLAN™

MY **APPOINTMENT** TRACKER™

MY **HABIT** TRANSFORMER™

MY **VISION** BOARD™

Review page 18–19

MY **BEFORE NOON** COMMITMENTS™

MY **DAILY PAGE** PLATFORM™

MY **NOTE** KEEPER™

Love WATER

LIFE PURPOSE PLAYBOOK

M TU W TH F SA SU DATE _____

MY **DAILY PAGE** PLATFORM™

MY **BEFORE NOON** COMMITMENTS™

am

MY **CELEBRATION** EXPERIENCE™

MY **GRATITUDE** EXPANDER™

MY **DAILY** INTENTION™

MY **TO-DO** GAMEPLAN™

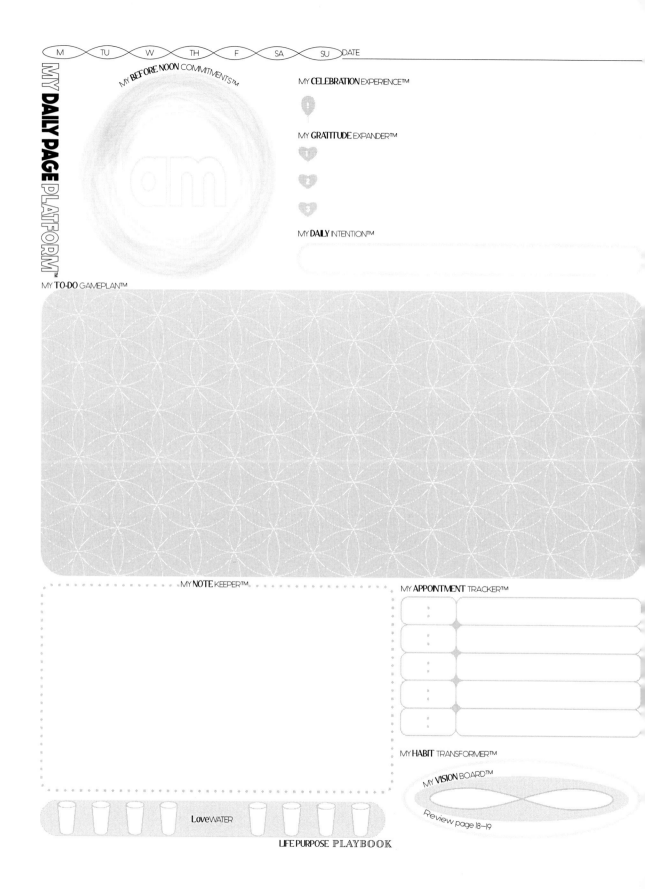

MY **NOTE** KEEPER™

MY **APPOINTMENT** TRACKER™

MY **HABIT** TRANSFORMER™

MY **VISION** BOARD™

Review page 18–19

Love WATER

LIFE PURPOSE PLAYBOOK

DATE _____ | M | TU | W | TH | F | SA | SU

MY **CELEBRATION** EXPERIENCE™

MY **GRATITUDE** EXPANDER™

MY **DAILY** INTENTION™

MY **TO-DO** GAMEPLAN™

MY BEFORE **NOON** COMMITMENTS™

MY **DAILY PAGE** PLATFORM™

MY **APPOINTMENT** TRACKER™

MY **NOTE** KEEPER™

MY **HABIT** TRANSFORMER™

MY **VISION** BOARD™

Review page 18–19

Love WATER

LIFE PURPOSE PLAYBOOK

MY **DAILY PAGE** PLATFORM™

MY BEFORE NOON COMMITMENTS™

MY **CELEBRATION** EXPERIENCE™

MY **GRATITUDE** EXPANDER™

MY **DAILY** INTENTION™

MY **TO-DO** GAMEPLAN™

MY **NOTE** KEEPER™

MY **APPOINTMENT** TRACKER™

MY **HABIT** TRANSFORMER™

MY **VISION** BOARD™

Review page 18–19

Love WATER

LIFE PURPOSE PLAYBOOK

MY WEEKLY CELEBRATION EXPERIENCE™

MY **OVERFLOW** TASKS™

MY
LIFE VISION
REVIEW™

Add the dates to the next 7 pages of
MY DAILY PAGE PLATFORM™.

Now review the following sections of this playbook
& transfer any tasks or projects into those 7 pages.

Any that are not urgent for this week should be
scheduled into MY OVERFLOW TASKS
on the NEXT **WEEKLY CHECK-IN.**

MY LIFE INTENTION MATRIX™
(page 14)

MY CIRCLE OF LIFE EXPANDER™
(page 21)

MY GOAL CHARTING SYSTEM™
(page 24–25)

MY IDEA & PROJECT MAGNIFIER™
(page 26–27)

MY TO-DO CHECKLIST™
(page 28–29)

MY YEAR AHEAD OUTLOOK™
(page 31)

MY MONTHLY PLANNER™
(page 32–55)

MY **3 MUST-DO's** THIS WEEK™

MY **DAILY PAGE** PLATFORM™

MY **BEFORE NOON** COMMITMENTS™

am

MY **CELEBRATION** EXPERIENCE™

MY **GRATITUDE** EXPANDER™

MY **DAILY** INTENTION™

MY **TO-DO** GAMEPLAN™

MY **NOTE** KEEPER™

MY **APPOINTMENT** TRACKER™

MY **HABIT** TRANSFORMER™

MY **VISION** BOARD™

Review page 18–19

Love WATER

LIFE PURPOSE PLAYBOOK

DATE _____ | M | TU | W | TH | F | SA | SU |

MY **CELEBRATION** EXPERIENCE™

MY **GRATITUDE** EXPANDER™

MY **DAILY** INTENTION™

MY **TO-DO** GAMEPLAN™

MY **BEFORE NOON** COMMITMENTS™

MY **DAILY PAGE** PLATFORM™

MY **APPOINTMENT** TRACKER™

MY **NOTE** KEEPER™

MY **HABIT** TRANSFORMER™

MY **VISION** BOARD™

Review page 18–19

Love WATER

LIFE PURPOSE PLAYBOOK

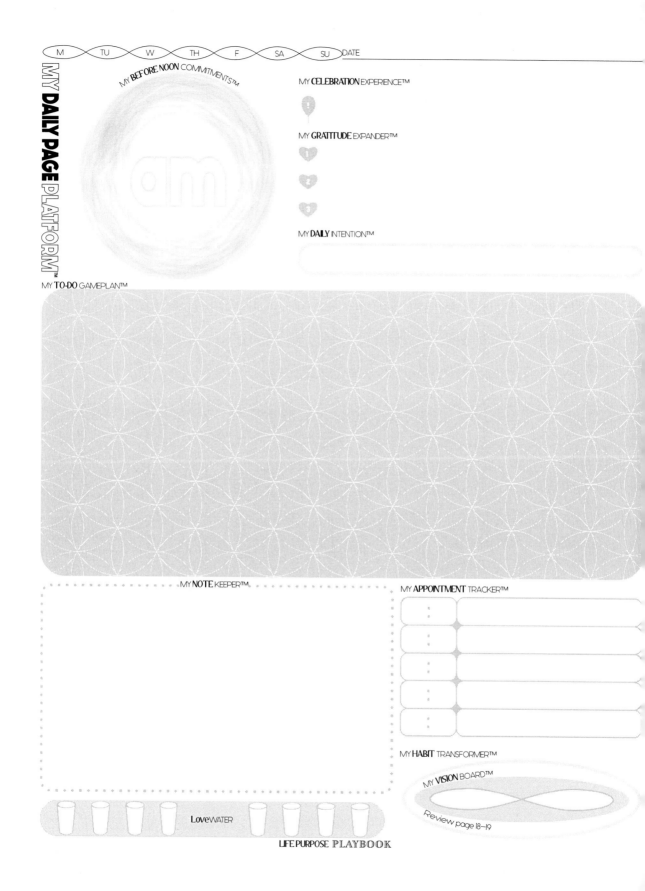

M TU W TH F SA SU DATE _____

MY DAILY PAGE PLATFORM™

MY *BEFORE NOON* COMMITMENTS™

MY **CELEBRATION** EXPERIENCE™

MY **GRATITUDE** EXPANDER™

MY **DAILY** INTENTION™

MY **TO-DO** GAMEPLAN™

MY **NOTE** KEEPER™

MY **APPOINTMENT** TRACKER™

MY **HABIT** TRANSFORMER™

MY **VISION** BOARD™

Review page 18—19

Love WATER

LIFE PURPOSE PLAYBOOK

DATE _____ | M | TU | W | TH | F | SA | SU |

MY **CELEBRATION** EXPERIENCE™

MY **GRATITUDE** EXPANDER™

MY **DAILY** INTENTION™

MY **TO-DO** GAMEPLAN™

MY BEFORE **NOON** COMMITMENTS™

MY **DAILY PAGE** PLATFORM™

MY **APPOINTMENT** TRACKER™

MY **NOTE** KEEPER™

MY **HABIT** TRANSFORMER™

MY **VISION** BOARD™

Review page 18–19

Love WATER

LIFE PURPOSE PLAYBOOK

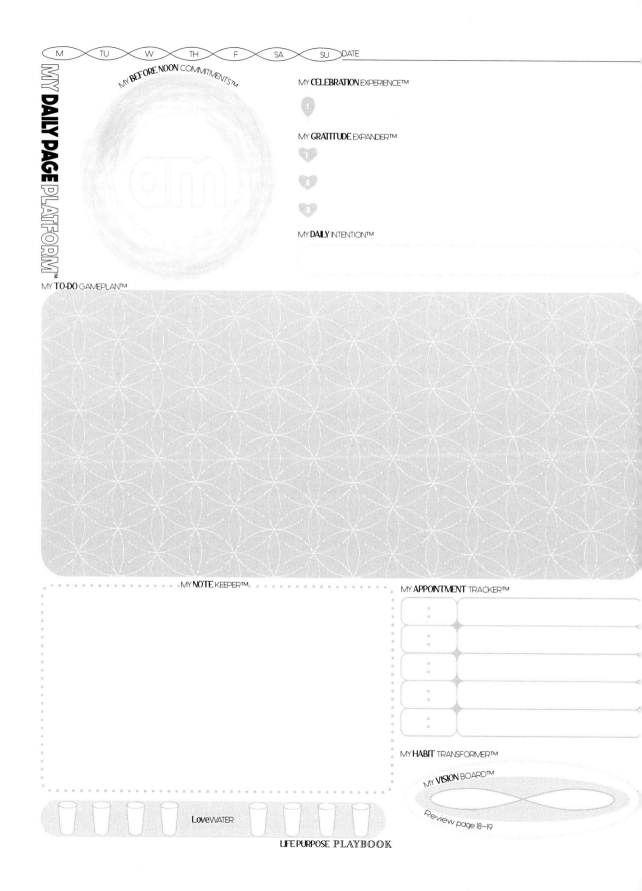

M | TU | W | TH | F | SA | SU | DATE _____

MY **DAILY PAGE** PLATFORM™

MY **BEFORE NOON** COMMITMENTS™

MY **CELEBRATION** EXPERIENCE™

MY **GRATITUDE** EXPANDER™

MY **DAILY** INTENTION™

MY **TO-DO** GAMEPLAN™

MY **NOTE** KEEPER™

MY **APPOINTMENT** TRACKER™

MY **HABIT** TRANSFORMER™

MY **VISION** BOARD™

Review page 18—19

Love WATER

LIFE PURPOSE PLAYBOOK

DATE _____ | M | TU | W | TH | F | SA | SU

MY **CELEBRATION** EXPERIENCE™

MY **GRATITUDE** EXPANDER™

MY **DAILY** INTENTION™

MY **TO-DO** GAMEPLAN™

MY BEFORE **NOON** COMMITMENTS™

MY **APPOINTMENT** TRACKER™

MY **NOTE** KEEPER™

MY **HABIT** TRANSFORMER™

MY **VISION** BOARD™

Review page 18–19

LoveWATER

LIFE PURPOSE PLAYBOOK

MY DAILY PAGE PLATFORM™

| M | TU | W | TH | F | SA | SU | DATE |

MY *BEFORE NOON* COMMITMENTS™

am

MY *CELEBRATION* EXPERIENCE™

MY *GRATITUDE* EXPANDER™

MY *DAILY* INTENTION™

MY *TO-DO* GAMEPLAN™

MY *NOTE* KEEPER™

MY *APPOINTMENT* TRACKER™

MY *HABIT* TRANSFORMER™

MY *VISION* BOARD™

Review page 18—19

LoveWATER

LIFE PURPOSE PLAYBOOK

MY **WEEKLY** CELEBRATION EXPERIENCE™

MY OVERFLOW TASKS™

MY
LIFE VISION
REVIEW™

Add the dates to the next 7 pages of
MY DAILY PAGE PLATFORM™.

Now review the following sections of this playbook
& transfer any tasks or projects into those 7 pages.

Any that are not urgent for this week should be
scheduled into MY OVERFLOW TASKS
on the NEXT **WEEKLY CHECK-IN.**

MY LIFE INTENTION MATRIX™
(page 14)

MY CIRCLE OF LIFE EXPANDER™
(page 21)

MY GOAL CHARTING SYSTEM™
(page 24–25)

MY IDEA & PROJECT MAGNIFIER™
(page 26–27)

MY TO-DO CHECKLIST™
(page 28–29)

MY YEAR AHEAD OUTLOOK™
(page 31)

MY MONTHLY PLANNER™
(page 32–55)

MY 3 MUST-DO'S THIS WEEK™

M | TU | W | TH | F | SA | SU | DATE _____

MY DAILY PAGE PLATFORM™

MY **BEFORE NOON** COMMITMENTS™

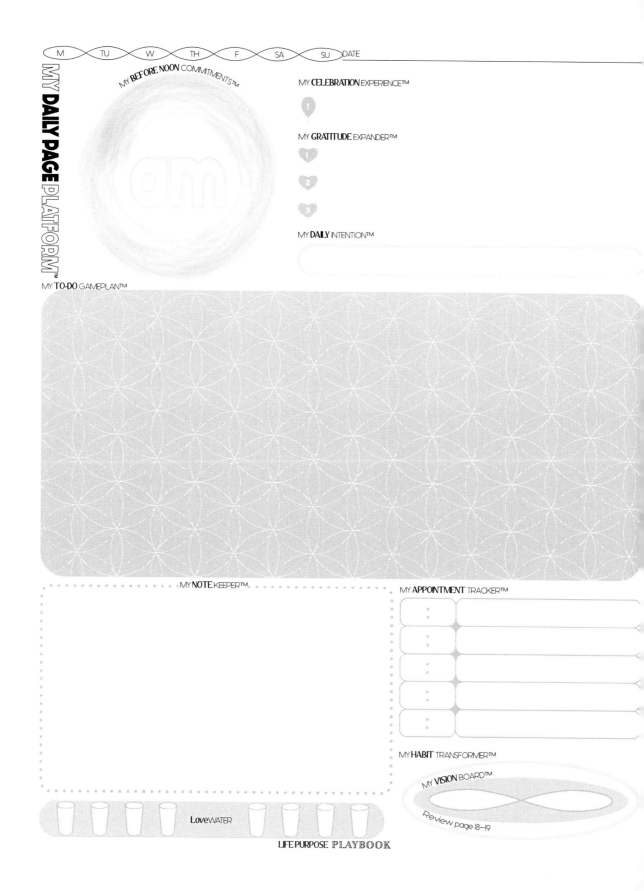

MY **CELEBRATION** EXPERIENCE™

MY **GRATITUDE** EXPANDER™

MY **DAILY** INTENTION™

MY **TO-DO** GAMEPLAN™

MY **NOTE** KEEPER™

MY **APPOINTMENT** TRACKER™

MY **HABIT** TRANSFORMER™

MY **VISION** BOARD™

Review page 18–19

Love WATER

LIFE PURPOSE PLAYBOOK

DATE _____ | M | TU | W | TH | F | SA | SU

MY **CELEBRATION** EXPERIENCE™

MY **GRATITUDE** EXPANDER™

MY **DAILY** INTENTION™

MY **TO-DO** GAMEPLAN™

MY BEFORE **NOON** COMMITMENTS™

MY **DAILY PAGE** PLATFORM™

MY **APPOINTMENT** TRACKER™

MY **NOTE** KEEPER™

MY **HABIT** TRANSFORMER™

MY **VISION** BOARD™

Review page 18–19

Love WATER

LIFE PURPOSE PLAYBOOK

MY DAILY PAGE PLATFORM™

M | TU | W | TH | F | SA | SU | DATE _____

MY BEFORE NOON COMMITMENTS™

am

MY CELEBRATION EXPERIENCE™

MY GRATITUDE EXPANDER™

MY DAILY INTENTION™

MY TO-DO GAMEPLAN™

MY NOTE KEEPER™

MY APPOINTMENT TRACKER™

MY HABIT TRANSFORMER™

MY VISION BOARD™

Review page 18–19

Love WATER

LIFE PURPOSE PLAYBOOK

DATE _____ M TU W TH F SA SU

MY **CELEBRATION** EXPERIENCE™

MY **GRATITUDE** EXPANDER™

MY **DAILY** INTENTION™

MY **TO-DO** GAMEPLAN™

MY **BEFORE NOON** COMMITMENTS™

MY **DAILY PAGE PLATFORM**™

MY **APPOINTMENT** TRACKER™

MY **NOTE** KEEPER™

MY **HABIT** TRANSFORMER™

MY **VISION** BOARD™

Review page 18–19

Love WATER

LIFE PURPOSE PLAYBOOK

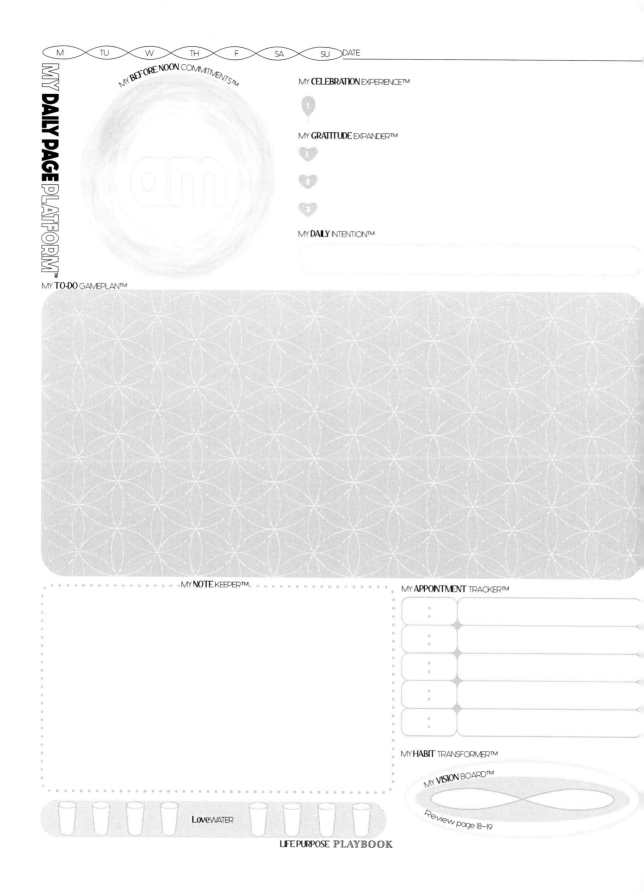

M | TU | W | TH | F | SA | SU | DATE

MY DAILY PAGE PLATFORM™

MY *BEFORE NOON* COMMITMENTS™

MY **CELEBRATION** EXPERIENCE™

MY **GRATITUDE** EXPANDER™

MY **DAILY** INTENTION™

MY **TO-DO** GAMEPLAN™

MY **NOTE** KEEPER™

MY **APPOINTMENT** TRACKER™

MY **HABIT** TRANSFORMER™

MY **VISION** BOARD™

Review page 18–19

LoveWATER

LIFE PURPOSE PLAYBOOK

DATE _____ | M | TU | W | TH | F | SA | SU |

MY **CELEBRATION** EXPERIENCE™

MY **GRATITUDE** EXPANDER™

MY **DAILY** INTENTION™

MY **TO-DO** GAMEPLAN™

MY BEFORE **NOON** COMMITMENTS™

MY DAILY PAGE PLATFORM™

MY **APPOINTMENT** TRACKER™

MY **NOTE** KEEPER™

MY **HABIT** TRANSFORMER™

MY **VISION** BOARD™

Review page 18–19

Love WATER

LIFE PURPOSE PLAYBOOK

MY DAILY PAGE PLATFORM™

MY *BEFORE NOON* COMMITMENTS™

MY *CELEBRATION* EXPERIENCE™

MY *GRATITUDE* EXPANDER™

MY *DAILY* INTENTION™

MY *TO-DO* GAMEPLAN™

••• MY *NOTE* KEEPER™ •••

MY *APPOINTMENT* TRACKER™

MY *HABIT* TRANSFORMER™

MY *VISION* BOARD™

Review page 18–19

Love WATER

LIFE PURPOSE PLAYBOOK

MY WEEKLY CELEBRATION EXPERIENCE™

MY OVERFLOW TASKS™

MY
LIFE VISION
REVIEW™

Add the dates to the next 7 pages of
MY DAILY PAGE PLATFORM™.

Now review the following sections of this playbook
& transfer any tasks or projects into those 7 pages.

Any that are not urgent for this week should be
scheduled into MY OVERFLOW TASKS
on the NEXT **WEEKLY CHECK-IN.**

MY LIFE INTENTION MATRIX™
(page 14)

MY CIRCLE OF LIFE EXPANDER™
(page 21)

MY GOAL CHARTING SYSTEM™
(page 24—25)

MY IDEA & PROJECT MAGNIFIER™
(page 26—27)

MY TO-DO CHECKLIST™
(page 28—29)

MY YEAR AHEAD OUTLOOK™
(page 31)

MY MONTHLY PLANNER™
(page 32—55)

MY 3 MUST-DO's THIS WEEK™

MY **DAILY PAGE** PLATFORM™

MY *BEFORE NOON* COMMITMENTS™

MY **CELEBRATION** EXPERIENCE™

MY **GRATITUDE** EXPANDER™

MY **DAILY** INTENTION™

MY **TO-DO** GAMEPLAN™

MY **NOTE** KEEPER™

MY **APPOINTMENT** TRACKER™

MY **HABIT** TRANSFORMER™

MY **VISION** BOARD™

Review page 18–19

Love WATER

LIFE PURPOSE PLAYBOOK

DATE _____

| M | TU | W | TH | F | SA | SU |

MY **CELEBRATION** EXPERIENCE™

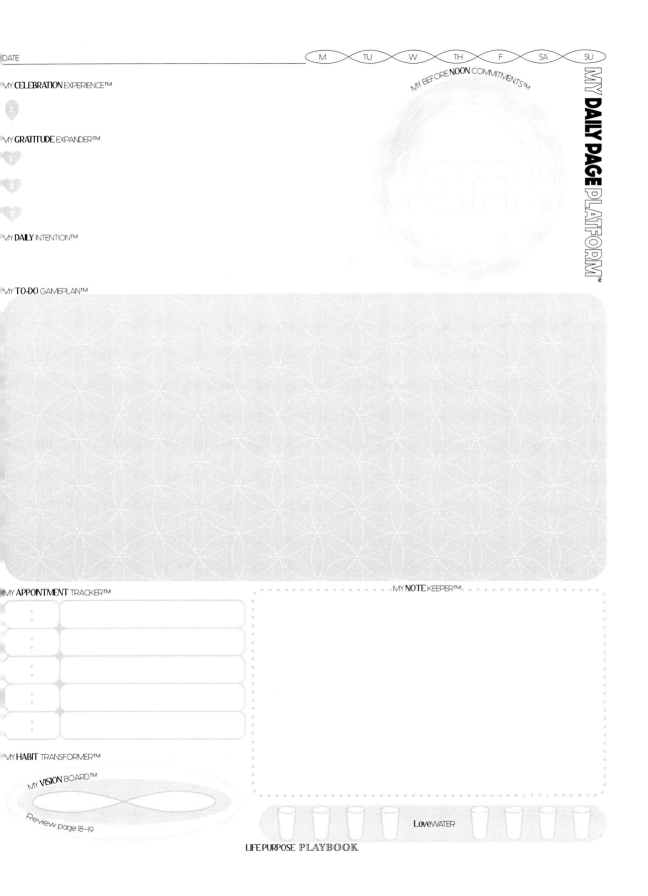

MY **GRATITUDE** EXPANDER™

MY **DAILY** INTENTION™

MY **TO-DO** GAMEPLAN™

MY BEFORE **NOON** COMMITMENTS™

MY **DAILY PAGE** PLATFORM™

MY **APPOINTMENT** TRACKER™

MY **NOTE** KEEPER™

MY **HABIT** TRANSFORMER™

MY **VISION** BOARD™

Review page 18–19

Love WATER

LIFE PURPOSE PLAYBOOK

MY **DAILY PAGE** PLATFORM™

MY **BEFORE NOON** COMMITMENTS™

MY **CELEBRATION** EXPERIENCE™

MY **GRATITUDE** EXPANDER™

MY **DAILY** INTENTION™

MY **TO-DO** GAMEPLAN™

MY **NOTE** KEEPER™

MY **APPOINTMENT** TRACKER™

MY **HABIT** TRANSFORMER™

MY **VISION** BOARD™

Review page 18—19

Love WATER

LIFE PURPOSE PLAYBOOK

DATE _____ | M | TU | W | TH | F | SA | SU |

MY **CELEBRATION** EXPERIENCE™

MY BEFORE **NOON** COMMITMENTS™

MY **GRATITUDE** EXPANDER™

MY **DAILY** INTENTION™

MY DAILY PAGE PLATFORM™

MY **TO-DO** GAMEPLAN™

MY **APPOINTMENT** TRACKER™

MY **NOTE** KEEPER™

MY **HABIT** TRANSFORMER™

MY **VISION** BOARD™

Review page 18–19

Love WATER

LIFE PURPOSE PLAYBOOK

MY **DAILY PAGE** PLATFORM™

MY **BEFORE NOON** COMMITMENTS™

MY **CELEBRATION** EXPERIENCE™

MY **GRATITUDE** EXPANDER™

MY **DAILY** INTENTION™

MY **TO-DO** GAMEPLAN™

MY **NOTE** KEEPER™

MY **APPOINTMENT** TRACKER™

MY **HABIT** TRANSFORMER™

MY **VISION** BOARD™

Review page 18–19

Love WATER

LIFE PURPOSE PLAYBOOK

DATE _____ M TU W TH F SA SU

MY **CELEBRATION** EXPERIENCE™

MY **GRATITUDE** EXPANDER™

MY **DAILY** INTENTION™

MY **TO-DO** GAMEPLAN™

MY BEFORE **NOON** COMMITMENTS™

MY **APPOINTMENT** TRACKER™

MY **NOTE** KEEPER™

MY **HABIT** TRANSFORMER™

MY **VISION** BOARD™

Review page 18–19

Love WATER

LIFE PURPOSE PLAYBOOK

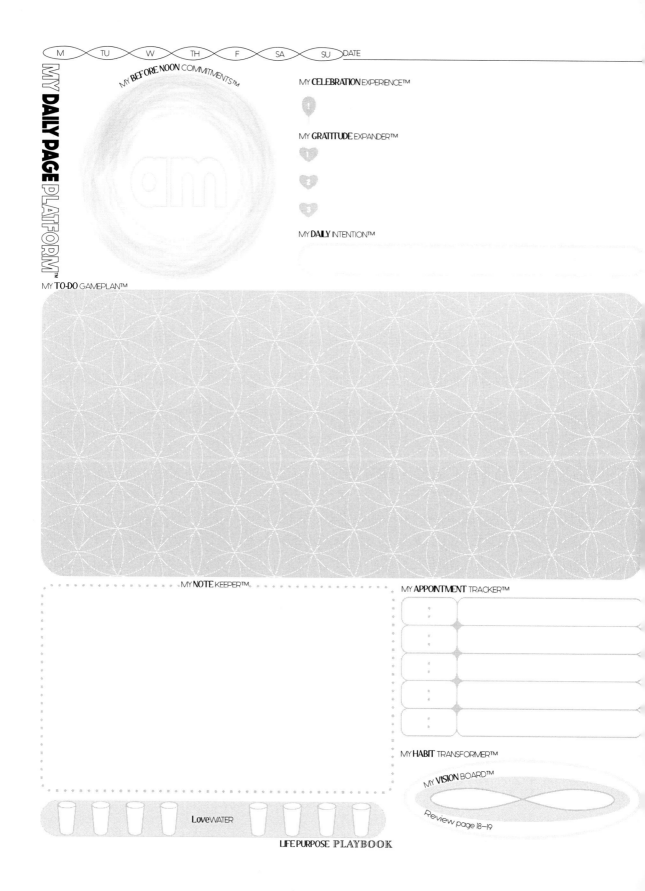

M | TU | W | TH | F | SA | SU | DATE

MY **DAILY PAGE** PLATFORM™

MY **BEFORE NOON** COMMITMENTS™

MY **CELEBRATION** EXPERIENCE™

MY **GRATITUDE** EXPANDER™

MY **DAILY** INTENTION™

MY **TO-DO** GAMEPLAN™

MY **NOTE** KEEPER™

MY **APPOINTMENT** TRACKER™

MY **HABIT** TRANSFORMER™

MY **VISION** BOARD™

Review page 18–19

Love WATER

LIFE PURPOSE PLAYBOOK

MY OVERFLOW TASKS™

MY WEEKLY CELEBRATION EXPERIENCE™

MY
LIFE VISION
REVIEW™

Add the dates to the next 7 pages of
MY DAILY PAGE PLATFORM™.

Now review the following sections of this playbook
& transfer any tasks or projects into those 7 pages.

Any that are not urgent for this week should be
scheduled into MY OVERFLOW TASKS
on the NEXT **WEEKLY CHECK-IN.**

MY LIFE INTENTION MATRIX™
(page 14)

MY CIRCLE OF LIFE EXPANDER™
(page 21)

MY GOAL CHARTING SYSTEM™
(page 24–25)

MY IDEA & PROJECT MAGNIFIER™
(page 26–27)

MY TO-DO CHECKLIST™
(page 28–29)

MY YEAR AHEAD OUTLOOK™
(page 31)

MY MONTHLY PLANNER™
(page 32–55)

MY 3 MUST-DO'S THIS WEEK™

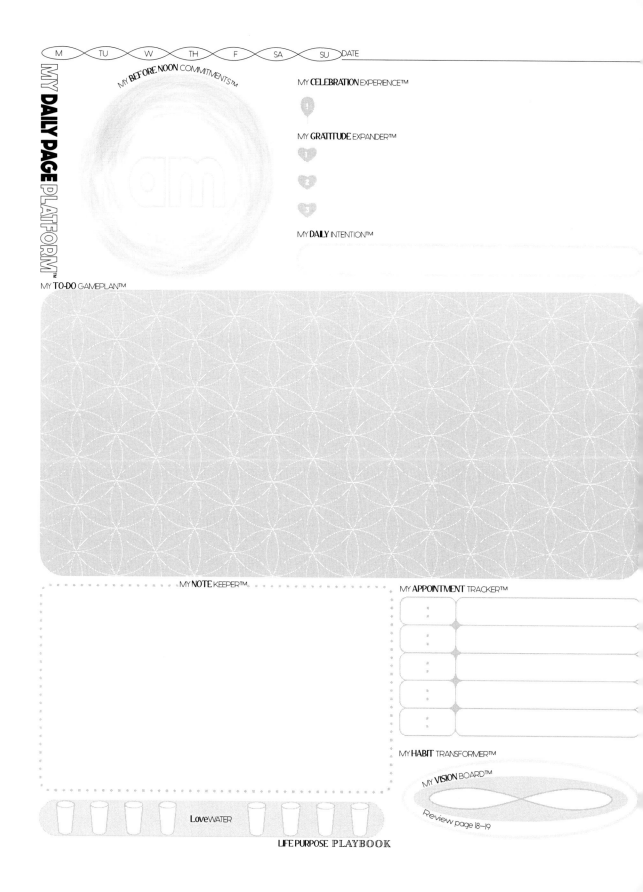

M   TU   W   TH   F   SA   SU   DATE _____

MY **DAILY PAGE** PLATFORM™

MY BEFORE NOON COMMITMENTS™

MY **CELEBRATION** EXPERIENCE™

MY **GRATITUDE** EXPANDER™

MY **DAILY** INTENTION™

MY **TO-DO** GAMEPLAN™

MY **NOTE** KEEPER™

MY **APPOINTMENT** TRACKER™

MY **HABIT** TRANSFORMER™

MY **VISION** BOARD™

Review page 18–19

Love WATER

LIFE PURPOSE PLAYBOOK

DATE _____ | M | TU | W | TH | F | SA | SU |

MY **CELEBRATION** EXPERIENCE™

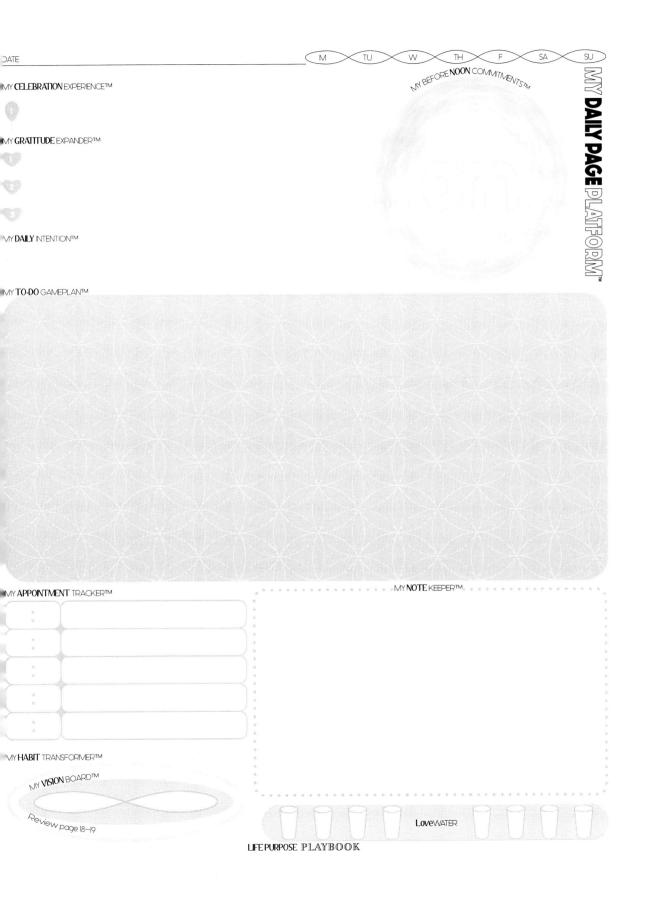

MY **BEFORE NOON** COMMITMENTS™

MY **GRATITUDE** EXPANDER™

MY **DAILY** INTENTION™

MY **TO-DO** GAMEPLAN™

MY **APPOINTMENT** TRACKER™

MY **NOTE** KEEPER™

MY **HABIT** TRANSFORMER™

MY **VISION** BOARD™

Review page 18–19

Love WATER

LIFE PURPOSE PLAYBOOK

MY **DAILY PAGE** PLATFORM™

M   TU   W   TH   F   SA   SU   DATE _____

MY DAILY PAGE PLATFORM™

MY *BEFORE NOON* COMMITMENTS™

am

MY *CELEBRATION* EXPERIENCE™

MY *GRATITUDE* EXPANDER™

MY *DAILY* INTENTION™

MY *TO-DO* GAMEPLAN™

MY *NOTE* KEEPER™

MY *APPOINTMENT* TRACKER™

MY *HABIT* TRANSFORMER™

MY *VISION* BOARD™

Review page 18–19

Love WATER

LIFE PURPOSE PLAYBOOK

DATE _____ | M | TU | W | TH | F | SA | SU |

MY **CELEBRATION** EXPERIENCE™

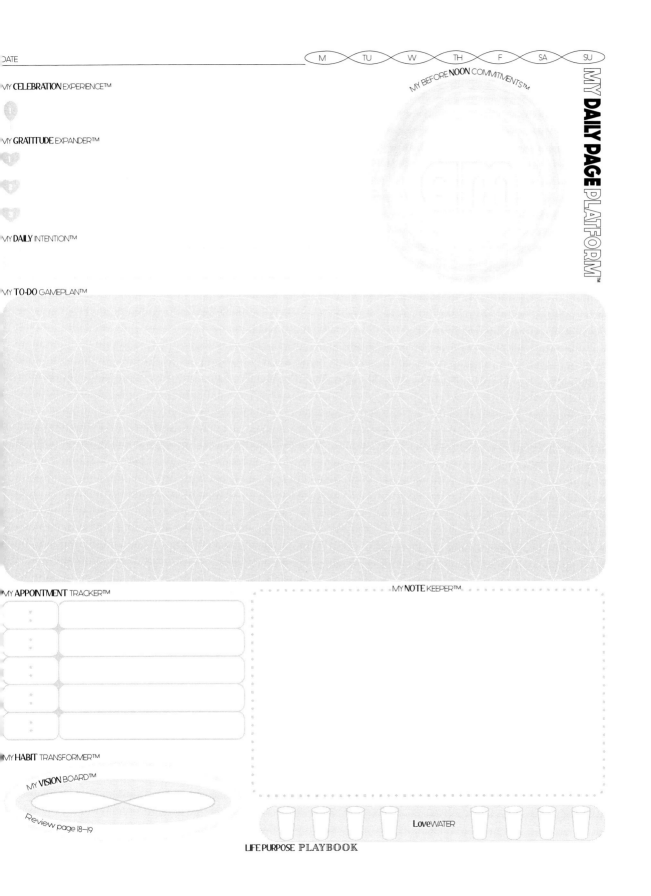

MY **GRATITUDE** EXPANDER™

MY **DAILY** INTENTION™

MY BEFORE **NOON** COMMITMENTS™

MY **TO-DO** GAMEPLAN™

MY **APPOINTMENT** TRACKER™

MY **NOTE** KEEPER™

MY **HABIT** TRANSFORMER™

MY **VISION** BOARD™

Review page 18–19

MY DAILY PAGE PLATFORM™

Love WATER

LIFE PURPOSE PLAYBOOK

MY **DAILY PAGE** PLATFORM™

MY *BEFORE NOON* COMMITMENTS™

am

MY **CELEBRATION** EXPERIENCE™

MY **GRATITUDE** EXPANDER™

MY **DAILY** INTENTION™

MY **TO-DO** GAMEPLAN™

MY **NOTE** KEEPER™

MY **APPOINTMENT** TRACKER™

MY **HABIT** TRANSFORMER™

MY **VISION** BOARD™

Review page 18—19

Love WATER

LIFE PURPOSE PLAYBOOK

DATE _____ M TU W TH F SA SU

MY **CELEBRATION** EXPERIENCE™

MY **GRATITUDE** EXPANDER™

MY **DAILY** INTENTION™

MY **TO-DO** GAMEPLAN™

MY BEFORE **NOON** COMMITMENTS™

MY **DAILY PAGE** PLATFORM™

MY **APPOINTMENT** TRACKER™

MY **NOTE** KEEPER™

MY **HABIT** TRANSFORMER™

MY **VISION** BOARD™

Review page 18–19

Love WATER

LIFE PURPOSE PLAYBOOK

MY **DAILY PAGE** PLATFORM™

MY **BEFORE NOON** COMMITMENTS™

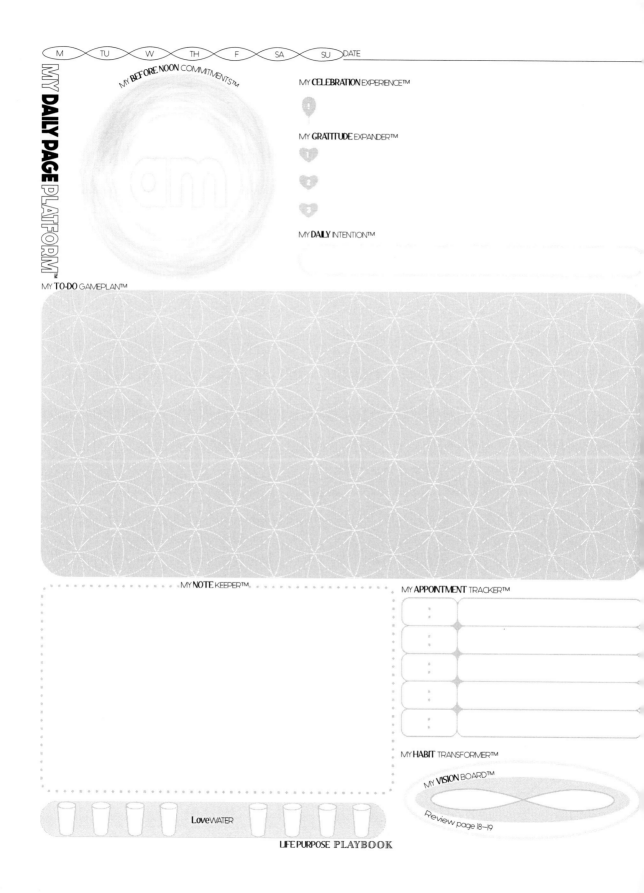

MY **CELEBRATION** EXPERIENCE™

MY **GRATITUDE** EXPANDER™

MY **DAILY** INTENTION™

MY **TO-DO** GAMEPLAN™

MY **NOTE** KEEPER™

MY **APPOINTMENT** TRACKER™

MY **HABIT** TRANSFORMER™

MY **VISION** BOARD™

Review page 18—19

Love WATER

LIFE PURPOSE PLAYBOOK

MY WEEKLY CELEBRATION EXPERIENCE™

MY OVERFLOW TASKS™

MY
LIFE VISION
REVIEW™

Add the dates to the next 7 pages of
MY DAILY PAGE PLATFORM™.

Now review the following sections of this playbook
& transfer any tasks or projects into those 7 pages.

Any that are not urgent for this week should be
scheduled into MY OVERFLOW TASKS
on the NEXT **WEEKLY CHECK-IN.**

MY LIFE INTENTION MATRIX™
(page 14)

MY CIRCLE OF LIFE EXPANDER™
(page 21)

MY GOAL CHARTING SYSTEM™
(page 24–25)

MY IDEA & PROJECT MAGNIFIER™
(page 26–27)

MY TO-DO CHECKLIST™
(page 28–29)

MY YEAR AHEAD OUTLOOK™
(page 31)

MY MONTHLY PLANNER™
(page 32–55)

MY 3 MUST-DO'S THIS WEEK™

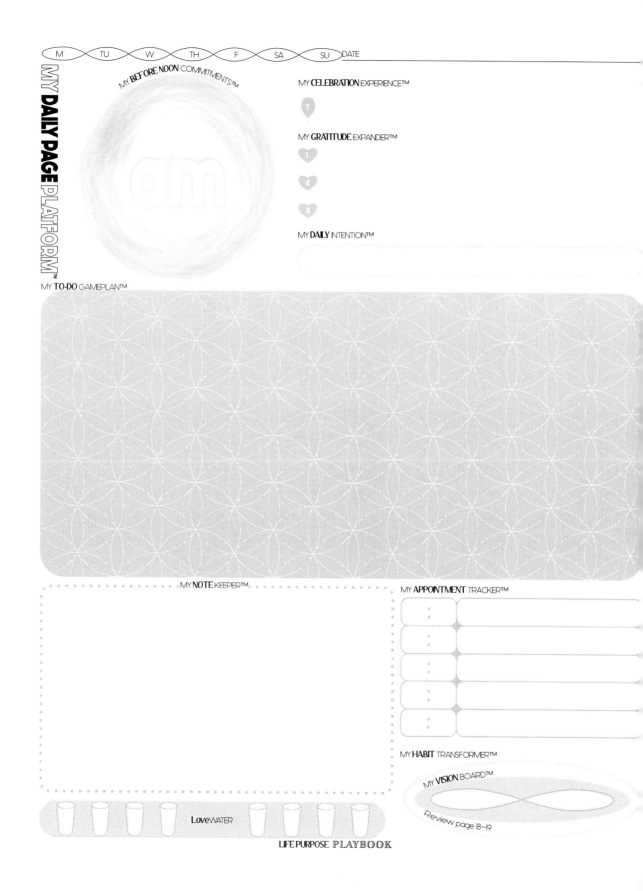

M | TU | W | TH | F | SA | SU | DATE

MY **DAILY PAGE** PLATFORM™

MY **BEFORE NOON** COMMITMENTS™

MY **CELEBRATION** EXPERIENCE™

MY **GRATITUDE** EXPANDER™

MY **DAILY** INTENTION™

MY **TO-DO** GAMEPLAN™

MY **NOTE** KEEPER™

MY **APPOINTMENT** TRACKER™

MY **HABIT** TRANSFORMER™

MY **VISION** BOARD™

Review page 18—19

Love WATER

LIFE PURPOSE PLAYBOOK

DATE _____ | M | TU | W | TH | F | SA | SU |

MY **CELEBRATION** EXPERIENCE™

MY **GRATITUDE** EXPANDER™

MY **DAILY** INTENTION™

MY **TO-DO** GAMEPLAN™

MY BEFORE **NOON** COMMITMENTS™

MY **APPOINTMENT** TRACKER™

MY **NOTE** KEEPER™

MY **HABIT** TRANSFORMER™

MY **VISION** BOARD™

Review page 18–19

Love WATER

LIFE PURPOSE PLAYBOOK

MY **DAILY PAGE** PLATFORM™

MY **BEFORE NOON** COMMITMENTS™

MY **CELEBRATION** EXPERIENCE™

MY **GRATITUDE** EXPANDER™

MY **DAILY** INTENTION™

MY **TO-DO** GAMEPLAN™

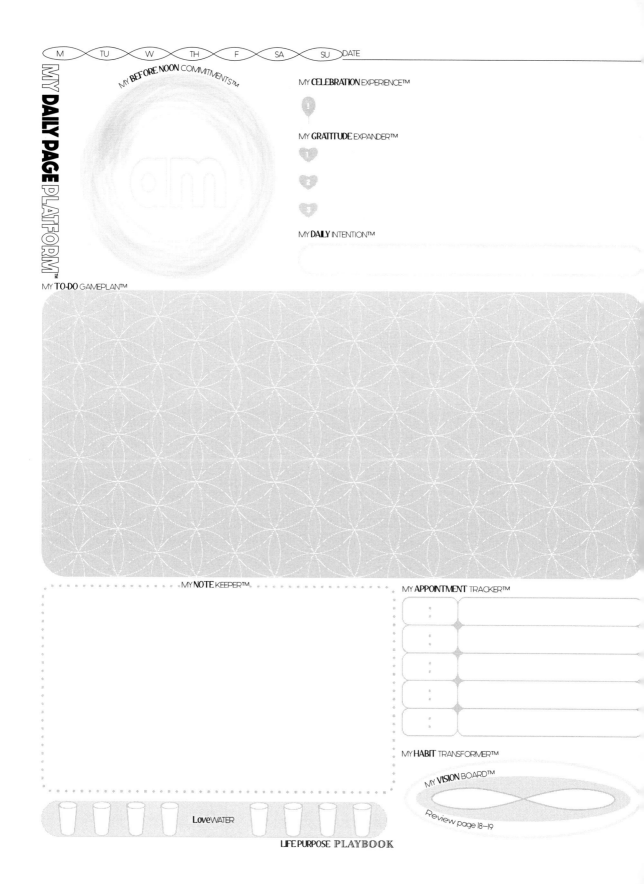

MY **NOTE** KEEPER™

MY **APPOINTMENT** TRACKER™

MY **HABIT** TRANSFORMER™

MY **VISION** BOARD™

Review page 18–19

Love WATER

LIFE PURPOSE PLAYBOOK

DATE _____ M | TU | W | TH | F | SA | SU

MY **CELEBRATION** EXPERIENCE™

MY **GRATITUDE** EXPANDER™

MY **DAILY** INTENTION™

MY **TO-DO** GAMEPLAN™

MY BEFORE **NOON** COMMITMENTS™

MY DAILY PAGE PLATFORM™

MY **APPOINTMENT** TRACKER™

·MY **NOTE** KEEPER™·

MY **HABIT** TRANSFORMER™

MY **VISION** BOARD™

Review page 18–19

Love WATER

LIFE PURPOSE PLAYBOOK

M | TU | W | TH | F | SA | SU | DATE _____

MY **DAILY PAGE** PLATFORM™

MY **BEFORE NOON** COMMITMENTS™

MY **CELEBRATION** EXPERIENCE™

MY **GRATITUDE** EXPANDER™

MY **DAILY** INTENTION™

MY **TO-DO** GAMEPLAN™

MY **NOTE** KEEPER™

MY **APPOINTMENT** TRACKER™

MY **HABIT** TRANSFORMER™

MY **VISION** BOARD™

Review page 18–19

Love WATER

LIFE PURPOSE PLAYBOOK

DATE _____ M TU W TH F SA SU

MY **CELEBRATION** EXPERIENCE™

MY **GRATITUDE** EXPANDER™

MY **DAILY** INTENTION™

MY BEFORE **NOON** COMMITMENTS™

MY DAILY PAGE PLATFORM™

MY **TO-DO** GAMEPLAN™

MY **APPOINTMENT** TRACKER™

MY **NOTE** KEEPER™

MY **HABIT** TRANSFORMER™

MY **VISION** BOARD™

Review page 18–19

LoveWATER

LIFE PURPOSE PLAYBOOK

M TU W TH F SA SU DATE _____

MY DAILY PAGE PLATFORM™

MY BEFORE NOON COMMITMENTS™

MY CELEBRATION EXPERIENCE™

MY GRATITUDE EXPANDER™

1

2

3

MY DAILY INTENTION™

MY TO-DO GAMEPLAN™

MY NOTE KEEPER™

MY APPOINTMENT TRACKER™

MY HABIT TRANSFORMER™

MY VISION BOARD™

Review page 18–19

Love WATER

LIFE PURPOSE PLAYBOOK

MY WEEKLY CELEBRATION EXPERIENCE™

MY OVERFLOW TASKS™

MY
LIFE VISION
REVIEW™

Add the dates to the next 7 pages of
MY DAILY PAGE PLATFORM™.

Now review the following sections of this playbook
& transfer any tasks or projects into those 7 pages.

Any that are not urgent for this week should be
scheduled into MY OVERFLOW TASKS
on the NEXT **WEEKLY CHECK-IN.**

MY LIFE INTENTION MATRIX™
(page 14)

MY CIRCLE OF LIFE EXPANDER™
(page 21)

MY GOAL CHARTING SYSTEM™
(page 24-25)

MY IDEA & PROJECT MAGNIFIER™
(page 26-27)

MY TO-DO CHECKLIST™
(page 28-29)

MY YEAR AHEAD OUTLOOK™
(page 31)

MY MONTHLY PLANNER™
(page 32-55)

MY 3 MUST-DO'S THIS WEEK™

M TU W TH F SA SU DATE _____

MY DAILY PAGE PLATFORM™

MY **BEFORE NOON** COMMITMENTS™

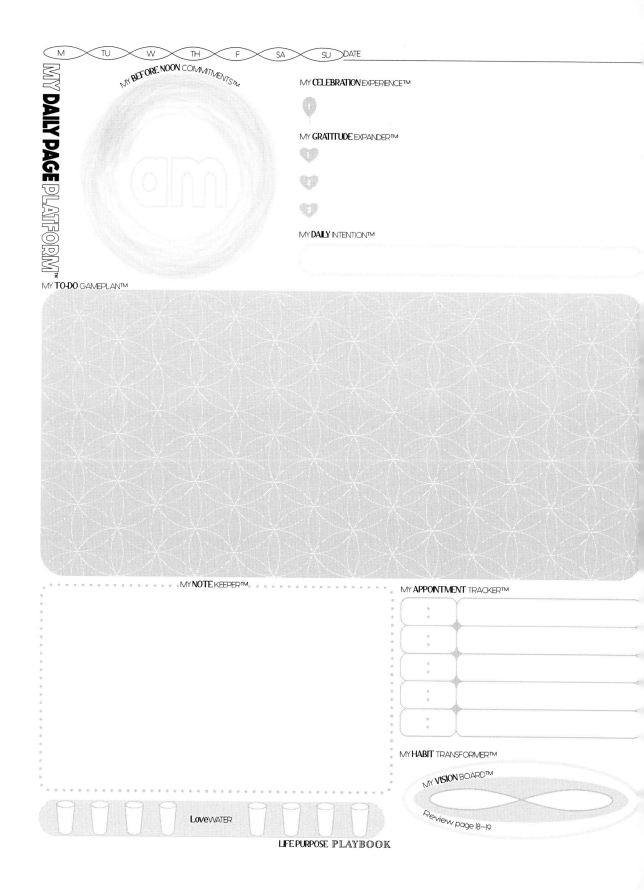

MY **CELEBRATION** EXPERIENCE™

MY **GRATITUDE** EXPANDER™

MY **DAILY** INTENTION™

MY **TO-DO** GAMEPLAN™

MY **NOTE** KEEPER™

MY **APPOINTMENT** TRACKER™

MY **HABIT** TRANSFORMER™

MY **VISION** BOARD™

Review page 18–19

Love WATER

LIFE PURPOSE PLAYBOOK

DATE _____ | M | TU | W | TH | F | SA | SU |

MY **CELEBRATION** EXPERIENCE™

MY **GRATITUDE** EXPANDER™

MY **DAILY** INTENTION™

MY **TO-DO** GAMEPLAN™

MY BEFORE **NOON** COMMITMENTS™

MY **APPOINTMENT** TRACKER™

MY **NOTE** KEEPER™

MY **HABIT** TRANSFORMER™

MY **VISION** BOARD™

Review page 18–19

Love WATER

LIFE PURPOSE PLAYBOOK

M | TU | W | TH | F | SA | SU | DATE

MY DAILY PAGE PLATFORM™

MY **BEFORE NOON** COMMITMENTS™

MY **CELEBRATION** EXPERIENCE™

MY **GRATITUDE** EXPANDER™

MY **DAILY** INTENTION™

MY **TO-DO** GAMEPLAN™

MY **NOTE** KEEPER™

MY **APPOINTMENT** TRACKER™

MY **HABIT** TRANSFORMER™

MY **VISION** BOARD™

Review page 18–19

Love WATER

LIFE PURPOSE PLAYBOOK

DATE _____ | M | TU | W | TH | F | SA | SU |

MY **CELEBRATION** EXPERIENCE™

MY **GRATITUDE** EXPANDER™

MY **DAILY** INTENTION™

MY BEFORE **NOON** COMMITMENTS™

MY DAILY PAGE PLATFORM™

MY **TO-DO** GAMEPLAN™

MY **APPOINTMENT** TRACKER™

MY **NOTE** KEEPER™

MY **HABIT** TRANSFORMER™

MY **VISION** BOARD™

Review page 18–19

LoveWATER

LIFE PURPOSE PLAYBOOK

MY DAILY PAGE PLATFORM™

M / TU / W / TH / F / SA / SU / DATE _____

MY **BEFORE NOON** COMMITMENTS™

MY **CELEBRATION** EXPERIENCE™

MY **GRATITUDE** EXPANDER™

1

2

3

MY **DAILY** INTENTION™

MY **TO-DO** GAMEPLAN™

MY **NOTE** KEEPER™

MY **APPOINTMENT** TRACKER™

MY **HABIT** TRANSFORMER™

MY **VISION** BOARD™

Review page 18–19

Love WATER

LIFE PURPOSE PLAYBOOK

DATE _____ | M | TU | W | TH | F | SA | SU |

MY **CELEBRATION** EXPERIENCE™

MY **GRATITUDE** EXPANDER™

MY **DAILY** INTENTION™

MY **TO-DO** GAMEPLAN™

MY BEFORE **NOON** COMMITMENTS™

MY **APPOINTMENT** TRACKER™

MY **NOTE** KEEPER™

MY **HABIT** TRANSFORMER™

MY **VISION** BOARD™

Review page 18–19

Love WATER

LIFE PURPOSE PLAYBOOK

MY DAILY PAGE PLATFORM™

M | TU | W | TH | F | SA | SU | DATE

MY DAILY PAGE PLATFORM™

MY *BEFORE NOON* COMMITMENTS™

MY *CELEBRATION* EXPERIENCE™

MY *GRATITUDE* EXPANDER™

MY *DAILY* INTENTION™

MY *TO-DO* GAMEPLAN™

MY *NOTE* KEEPER™

MY *APPOINTMENT* TRACKER™

MY *HABIT* TRANSFORMER™

MY *VISION* BOARD™

Review page 18—19

Love WATER

LIFE PURPOSE PLAYBOOK

MY WEEKLY CELEBRATION EXPERIENCE™

MY OVERFLOW TASKS™

MY
LIFE VISION
REVIEW™

Add the dates to the next 7 pages of
MY DAILY PAGE PLATFORM™.

Now review the following sections of this playbook
& transfer any tasks or projects into those 7 pages.

Any that are not urgent for this week should be
scheduled into MY OVERFLOW TASKS
on the NEXT **WEEKLY CHECK-IN.**

MY LIFE INTENTION MATRIX™
(page 14)

MY CIRCLE OF LIFE EXPANDER™
(page 21)

MY GOAL CHARTING SYSTEM™
(page 24–25)

MY IDEA & PROJECT MAGNIFIER™
(page 26–27)

MY TO-DO CHECKLIST™
(page 28–29)

MY YEAR AHEAD OUTLOOK™
(page 31)

MY MONTHLY PLANNER™
(page 32–55)

MY 3 MUST-DO'S THIS WEEK™

MY **DAILY PAGE** PLATFORM™

MY **BEFORE NOON** COMMITMENTS™

MY **CELEBRATION** EXPERIENCE™

MY **GRATITUDE** EXPANDER™

1

2

3

MY **DAILY** INTENTION™

MY **TO-DO** GAMEPLAN™

MY **NOTE** KEEPER™

MY **APPOINTMENT** TRACKER™

MY **HABIT** TRANSFORMER™

MY **VISION** BOARD™

Review page 18–19

Love WATER

LIFE PURPOSE PLAYBOOK

DATE _____ | M | TU | W | TH | F | SA | SU |

MY **CELEBRATION** EXPERIENCE™

MY **GRATITUDE** EXPANDER™

MY **DAILY** INTENTION™

MY **TO-DO** GAMEPLAN™

MY **APPOINTMENT** TRACKER™

MY **HABIT** TRANSFORMER™

MY **VISION** BOARD™

Review page 18–19

MY BEFORE **NOON** COMMITMENTS™

MY **NOTE** KEEPER™

LoveWATER

LIFE PURPOSE PLAYBOOK

MY **DAILY PAGE** PLATFORM™

MY **BEFORE NOON** COMMITMENTS™

MY **CELEBRATION** EXPERIENCE™

MY **GRATITUDE** EXPANDER™

MY **DAILY** INTENTION™

MY **TO-DO** GAMEPLAN™

MY **NOTE** KEEPER™

MY **APPOINTMENT** TRACKER™

MY **HABIT** TRANSFORMER™

MY **VISION** BOARD™

Review page 18—19

Love WATER

LIFE PURPOSE PLAYBOOK

DATE _____ M | TU | W | TH | F | SA | SU

MY **CELEBRATION** EXPERIENCE™

MY **BEFORE NOON** COMMITMENTS™

MY **GRATITUDE** EXPANDER™

MY **DAILY** INTENTION™

MY **TO-DO** GAMEPLAN™

MY **APPOINTMENT** TRACKER™

MY **NOTE** KEEPER™

MY **HABIT** TRANSFORMER™

MY **VISION** BOARD™

Review page 18–19

Love WATER

LIFE PURPOSE PLAYBOOK

MY **DAILY PAGE** PLATFORM™

M   TU   W   TH   F   SA   SU   DATE _____

MY **DAILY PAGE** PLATFORM™

MY **BEFORE NOON** COMMITMENTS™

MY **CELEBRATION** EXPERIENCE™

MY **GRATITUDE** EXPANDER™

MY **DAILY** INTENTION™

MY **TO-DO** GAMEPLAN™

MY **NOTE** KEEPER™

MY **APPOINTMENT** TRACKER™

MY **HABIT** TRANSFORMER™

MY **VISION** BOARD™

Review page 18–19

Love WATER

LIFE PURPOSE PLAYBOOK

DATE _____ M / TU / W / TH / F / SA / SU

MY **CELEBRATION** EXPERIENCE™

MY **GRATITUDE** EXPANDER™

MY **DAILY** INTENTION™

MY **TO-DO** GAMEPLAN™

MY BEFORE **NOON** COMMITMENTS™

MY **DAILY PAGE** PLATFORM™

MY **APPOINTMENT** TRACKER™

MY **NOTE** KEEPER™

MY **HABIT** TRANSFORMER™

MY **VISION** BOARD™

Review page 18–19

Love WATER

LIFE PURPOSE PLAYBOOK

MY DAILY PAGE PLATFORM™

M | TU | W | TH | F | SA | SU | DATE _____

MY **BEFORE NOON** COMMITMENTS™

MY **CELEBRATION** EXPERIENCE™

MY **GRATITUDE** EXPANDER™

MY **DAILY** INTENTION™

MY **TO-DO** GAMEPLAN™

MY **NOTE** KEEPER™

MY **APPOINTMENT** TRACKER™

MY **HABIT** TRANSFORMER™

MY **VISION** BOARD™

Review page 18—19

Love WATER

LIFE PURPOSE PLAYBOOK

MY **WEEKLY** CELEBRATION EXPERIENCE™

MY
OVERFLOW
TASKS™

MY
LIFE VISION
REVIEW™

Add the dates to the next 7 pages of
MY DAILY PAGE PLATFORM™.

Now review the following sections of this playbook
& transfer any tasks or projects into those 7 pages.

Any that are not urgent for this week should be
scheduled into MY OVERFLOW TASKS
on the NEXT **WEEKLY CHECK-IN.**

MY LIFE INTENTION MATRIX™
(page 14)

MY CIRCLE OF LIFE EXPANDER™
(page 21)

MY GOAL CHARTING SYSTEM™
(page 24–25)

MY IDEA & PROJECT MAGNIFIER™
(page 26–27)

MY TO-DO CHECKLIST™
(page 28–29)

MY YEAR AHEAD OUTLOOK™
(page 31)

MY MONTHLY PLANNER™
(page 32–55)

MY 3 MUST-DO's THIS WEEK™

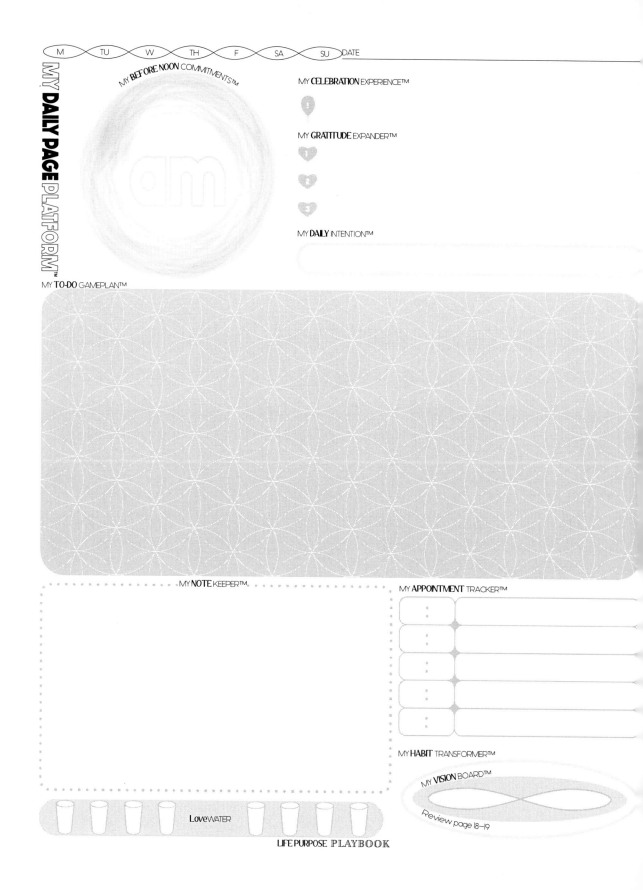

M | TU | W | TH | F | SA | SU | DATE

MY DAILY PAGE PLATFORM™

MY **BEFORE NOON** COMMITMENTS™

MY **CELEBRATION** EXPERIENCE™

MY **GRATITUDE** EXPANDER™

MY **DAILY** INTENTION™

MY **TO-DO** GAMEPLAN™

MY **NOTE** KEEPER™

MY **APPOINTMENT** TRACKER™

MY **HABIT** TRANSFORMER™

MY **VISION** BOARD™

Review page 18—19

Love WATER

LIFE PURPOSE PLAYBOOK

DATE _____ M TU W TH F SA SU

MY **CELEBRATION** EXPERIENCE™

MY **GRATITUDE** EXPANDER™

MY **DAILY** INTENTION™

MY **BEFORE NOON** COMMITMENTS™

MY **TO-DO** GAMEPLAN™

MY **DAILY PAGE** PLATFORM™

MY **APPOINTMENT** TRACKER™

MY **NOTE** KEEPER™

MY **HABIT** TRANSFORMER™

MY **VISION** BOARD™

Review page 18–19

Love WATER

LIFE PURPOSE PLAYBOOK

MY **DAILY PAGE** PLATFORM™

MY **BEFORE NOON** COMMITMENTS™

MY **CELEBRATION** EXPERIENCE™

MY **GRATITUDE** EXPANDER™

MY **DAILY** INTENTION™

MY **TO-DO** GAMEPLAN™

MY **NOTE** KEEPER™

MY **APPOINTMENT** TRACKER™

MY **HABIT** TRANSFORMER™

MY **VISION** BOARD™

Review page 18—19

Love WATER

LIFE PURPOSE PLAYBOOK

DATE _____

| M | TU | W | TH | F | SA | SU |

MY **CELEBRATION** EXPERIENCE™

MY **GRATITUDE** EXPANDER™

MY **DAILY** INTENTION™

MY **TO-DO** GAMEPLAN™

MY **BEFORE NOON** COMMITMENTS™

MY DAILY PAGE PLATFORM™

MY **APPOINTMENT** TRACKER™

MY **NOTE** KEEPER™

MY **HABIT** TRANSFORMER™

MY **VISION** BOARD™

Review page 18–19

Love WATER

LIFE PURPOSE PLAYBOOK

M   TU   W   TH   F   SA   SU   DATE _____

MY DAILY PAGE PLATFORM™

MY BEFORE NOON COMMITMENTS™

MY CELEBRATION EXPERIENCE™

MY GRATITUDE EXPANDER™

MY DAILY INTENTION™

MY TO-DO GAMEPLAN™

MY NOTE KEEPER™

MY APPOINTMENT TRACKER™

MY HABIT TRANSFORMER™

MY VISION BOARD™

Review page 18—19

Love WATER

LIFE PURPOSE PLAYBOOK

DATE _____

| M | TU | W | TH | F | SA | SU |

MY **CELEBRATION** EXPERIENCE™

MY **GRATITUDE** EXPANDER™

MY **DAILY** INTENTION™

MY **TO-DO** GAMEPLAN™

MY BEFORE **NOON** COMMITMENTS™

MY DAILY PAGE PLATFORM™

MY **APPOINTMENT** TRACKER™

MY **NOTE** KEEPER™

MY **HABIT** TRANSFORMER™

MY **VISION** BOARD™

Review page 18—19

LoveWATER

LIFE PURPOSE PLAYBOOK

M TU W TH F SA SU DATE _____

MY DAILY PAGE PLATFORM™

MY BEFORE NOON COMMITMENTS™

am

MY CELEBRATION EXPERIENCE™

MY GRATITUDE EXPANDER™

MY DAILY INTENTION™

MY TO-DO GAMEPLAN™

MY NOTE KEEPER™

MY APPOINTMENT TRACKER™

MY HABIT TRANSFORMER™

MY VISION BOARD™

Review page 18–19

Love WATER

LIFE PURPOSE PLAYBOOK

MY **WEEKLY** CELEBRATION EXPERIENCE™

MY
OVERFLOW
TASKS™

MY
LIFE VISION
REVIEW™

Add the dates to the next 7 pages of
MY DAILY PAGE PLATFORM™.

Now review the following sections of this playbook
& transfer any tasks or projects into those 7 pages.

Any that are not urgent for this week should be
scheduled into MY OVERFLOW TASKS
on the NEXT **WEEKLY CHECK-IN.**

MY LIFE INTENTION MATRIX™
(page 14)

MY CIRCLE OF LIFE EXPANDER™
(page 21)

MY GOAL CHARTING SYSTEM™
(page 24–25)

MY IDEA & PROJECT MAGNIFIER™
(page 26–27)

MY TO-DO CHECKLIST™
(page 28–29)

MY YEAR AHEAD OUTLOOK™
(page 31)

MY MONTHLY PLANNER™
(page 32–55)

MY 3 MUST-DO'S THIS WEEK™

MY DAILY PAGE PLATFORM™

MY **BEFORE NOON** COMMITMENTS™

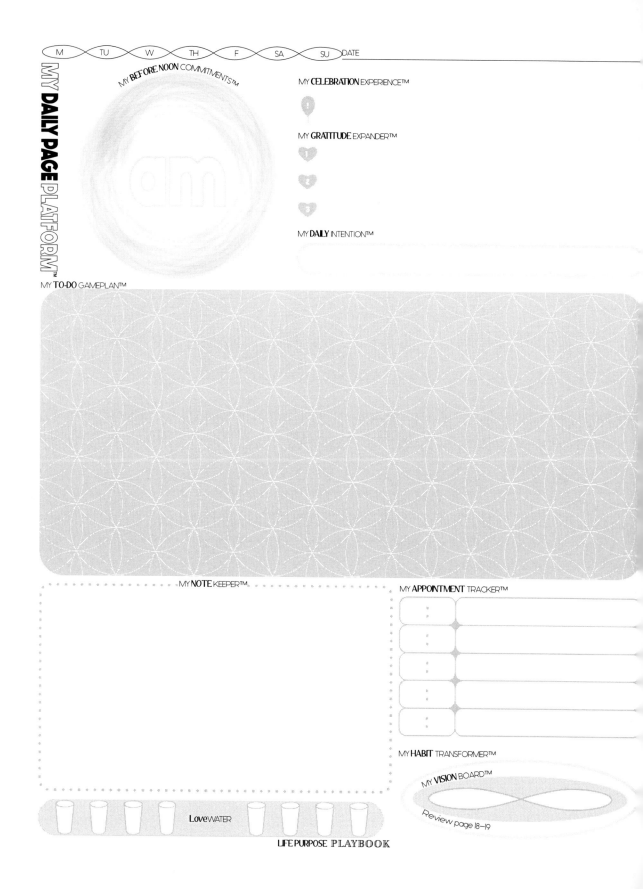

am

MY **CELEBRATION** EXPERIENCE™

MY **GRATITUDE** EXPANDER™

MY **DAILY** INTENTION™

MY **TO-DO** GAMEPLAN™

MY **NOTE** KEEPER™

MY **APPOINTMENT** TRACKER™

MY **HABIT** TRANSFORMER™

MY **VISION** BOARD™

Review page 18—19

Love WATER

LIFE PURPOSE PLAYBOOK

DATE _____ | M | TU | W | TH | F | SA | SU |

MY **CELEBRATION** EXPERIENCE™

MY BEFORE **NOON** COMMITMENTS™

MY **DAILY PAGE** PLATFORM™

MY **GRATITUDE** EXPANDER™

MY **DAILY** INTENTION™

MY **TO-DO** GAMEPLAN™

MY **APPOINTMENT** TRACKER™

MY **NOTE** KEEPER™

MY **HABIT** TRANSFORMER™

MY **VISION** BOARD™

Review page 18–19

Love WATER

LIFE PURPOSE PLAYBOOK

M | TU | W | TH | F | SA | SU | DATE _____

MY **DAILY PAGE** PLATFORM™

MY **BEFORE NOON** COMMITMENTS™

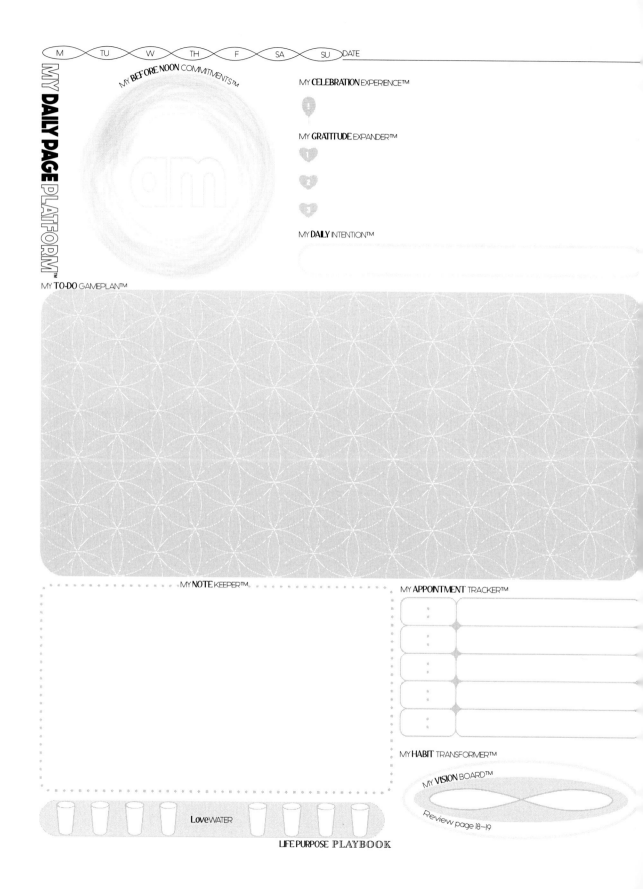

am

MY **CELEBRATION** EXPERIENCE™

MY **GRATITUDE** EXPANDER™

MY **DAILY** INTENTION™

MY **TO-DO** GAMEPLAN™

MY **NOTE** KEEPER™

MY **APPOINTMENT** TRACKER™

MY **HABIT** TRANSFORMER™

MY **VISION** BOARD™

Review page 18–19

LoveWATER

LIFE PURPOSE PLAYBOOK

DATE _____ | M | TU | W | TH | F | SA | SU |

MY **CELEBRATION** EXPERIENCE™

MY **GRATITUDE** EXPANDER™

MY **DAILY** INTENTION™

MY **TO-DO** GAMEPLAN™

MY BEFORE **NOON** COMMITMENTS™

MY **APPOINTMENT** TRACKER™

MY **NOTE** KEEPER™

MY **HABIT** TRANSFORMER™

MY **VISION** BOARD™

Review page 18—19

LoveWATER

LIFE PURPOSE PLAYBOOK

M | TU | W | TH | F | SA | SU | DATE

MY **DAILY PAGE** PLATFORM™

MY BEFORE NOON COMMITMENTS™

am

MY **CELEBRATION** EXPERIENCE™

MY **GRATITUDE** EXPANDER™

MY **DAILY** INTENTION™

MY **TO-DO** GAMEPLAN™

MY **NOTE** KEEPER™

MY **APPOINTMENT** TRACKER™

MY **HABIT** TRANSFORMER™

MY **VISION** BOARD™

Review page 18—19

Love WATER

LIFE PURPOSE PLAYBOOK

DATE _____ | M | TU | W | TH | F | SA | SU

MY **CELEBRATION** EXPERIENCE™

MY **GRATITUDE** EXPANDER™

MY **DAILY** INTENTION™

MY BEFORE **NOON** COMMITMENTS™

MY **TO-DO** GAMEPLAN™

MY **APPOINTMENT** TRACKER™

MY **NOTE** KEEPER™

MY **HABIT** TRANSFORMER™

MY **VISION** BOARD™

Review page 18–19

Love WATER

LIFE PURPOSE PLAYBOOK

M | TU | W | TH | F | SA | SU | DATE

MY **DAILY PAGE** PLATFORM™

MY **BEFORE NOON** COMMITMENTS™

MY **CELEBRATION** EXPERIENCE™

MY **GRATITUDE** EXPANDER™

MY **DAILY** INTENTION™

MY **TO-DO** GAMEPLAN™

MY **NOTE** KEEPER™

MY **APPOINTMENT** TRACKER™

MY **HABIT** TRANSFORMER™

MY **VISION** BOARD™

Review page 18–19

Love WATER

LIFE PURPOSE PLAYBOOK

MY WEEKLY CELEBRATION EXPERIENCE™

MY
OVERFLOW
TASKS™

MY
LIFE VISION
REVIEW™

Add the dates to the next 7 pages of
MY DAILY PAGE PLATFORM™.

Now review the following sections of this playbook
& transfer any tasks or projects into those 7 pages.

Any that are not urgent for this week should be
scheduled into MY OVERFLOW TASKS
on the NEXT **WEEKLY CHECK-IN.**

MY LIFE INTENTION MATRIX™
(page 14)

MY CIRCLE OF LIFE EXPANDER™
(page 21)

MY GOAL CHARTING SYSTEM™
(page 24–25)

MY IDEA & PROJECT MAGNIFIER™
(page 26–27)

MY TO-DO CHECKLIST™
(page 28–29)

MY YEAR AHEAD OUTLOOK™
(page 31)

MY MONTHLY PLANNER™
(page 32–55)

MY 3 MUST-DO's THIS WEEK™

M TU W TH F SA SU DATE _____

MY DAILY PAGE PLATFORM™

MY BEFORE NOON COMMITMENTS™

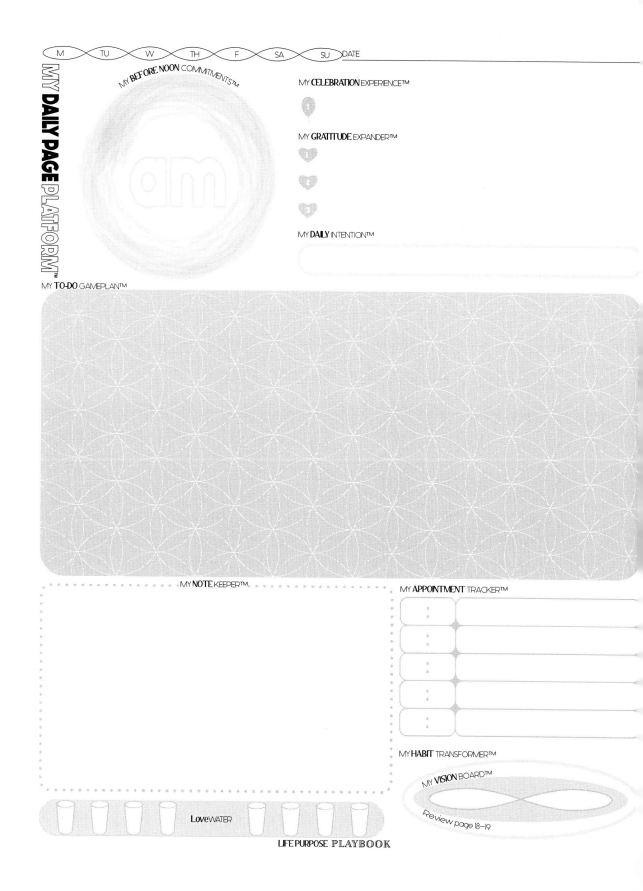

MY CELEBRATION EXPERIENCE™

MY GRATITUDE EXPANDER™

MY DAILY INTENTION™

MY TO-DO GAMEPLAN™

MY NOTE KEEPER™

MY APPOINTMENT TRACKER™

MY HABIT TRANSFORMER™

MY VISION BOARD™

Review page 18–19

Love WATER

LIFE PURPOSE PLAYBOOK

DATE _____

| M | TU | W | TH | F | SA | SU |

MY **CELEBRATION** EXPERIENCE™

MY **GRATITUDE** EXPANDER™

MY **DAILY** INTENTION™

MY BEFORE **NOON** COMMITMENTS™

MY **TO-DO** GAMEPLAN™

MY **APPOINTMENT** TRACKER™

MY **NOTE** KEEPER™

MY **HABIT** TRANSFORMER™

MY **VISION** BOARD™

Review page 18–19

Love WATER

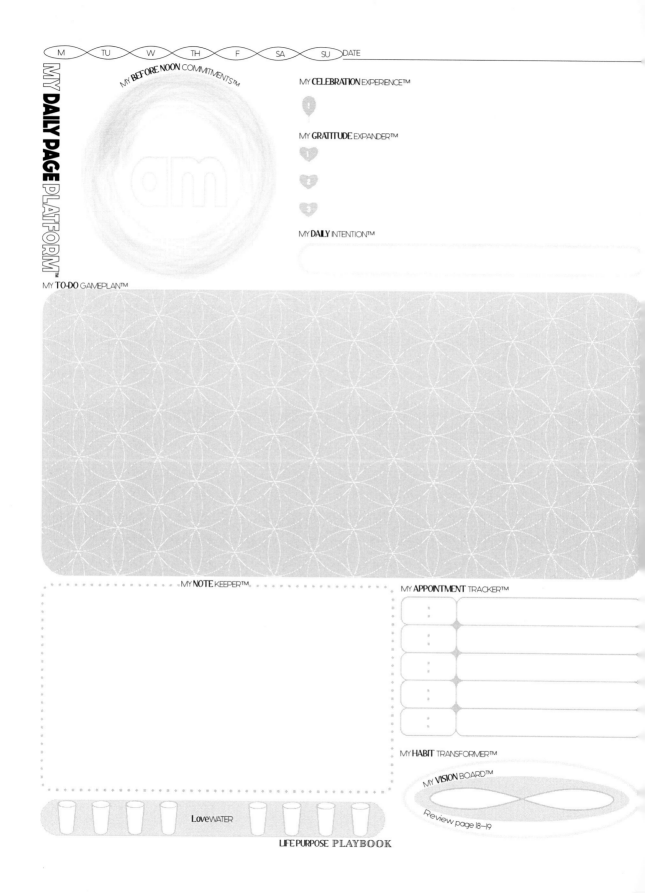

M / TU / W / TH / F / SA / SU / DATE _____

MY **DAILY PAGE** PLATFORM™

MY **BEFORE NOON** COMMITMENTS™

am

MY **TO-DO** GAMEPLAN™

MY **CELEBRATION** EXPERIENCE™

MY **GRATITUDE** EXPANDER™

MY **DAILY** INTENTION™

MY **NOTE** KEEPER™

MY **APPOINTMENT** TRACKER™

MY **HABIT** TRANSFORMER™

MY **VISION** BOARD™

Review page 18–19

Love WATER

LIFE PURPOSE PLAYBOOK

DATE _____

| M | TU | W | TH | F | SA | SU |

MY **CELEBRATION** EXPERIENCE™

MY BEFORE **NOON** COMMITMENTS™

MY **GRATITUDE** EXPANDER™

MY **DAILY** INTENTION™

MY **TO-DO** GAMEPLAN™

MY **APPOINTMENT** TRACKER™

MY **NOTE** KEEPER™

MY **HABIT** TRANSFORMER™

MY **VISION** BOARD™

Review page 18–19

Love WATER

LIFE PURPOSE PLAYBOOK

MY **DAILY PAGE** PLATFORM™

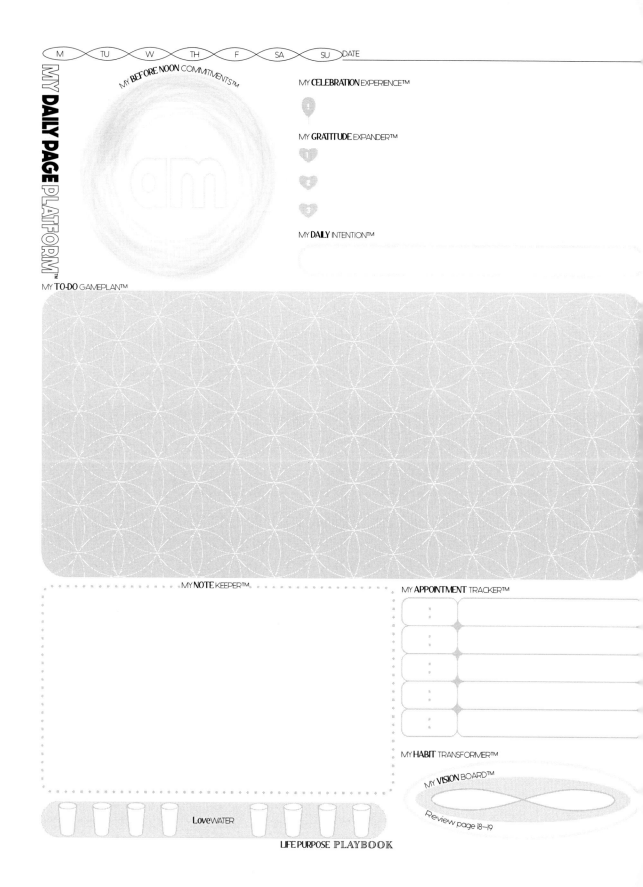

M | TU | W | TH | F | SA | SU | DATE _____

MY **DAILY PAGE** PLATFORM™

MY **BEFORE NOON** COMMITMENTS™

MY **CELEBRATION** EXPERIENCE™

MY **GRATITUDE** EXPANDER™

MY **DAILY** INTENTION™

MY **TO-DO** GAMEPLAN™

MY **NOTE** KEEPER™

MY **APPOINTMENT** TRACKER™

MY **HABIT** TRANSFORMER™

MY **VISION** BOARD™

Review page 18–19

Love WATER

LIFE PURPOSE PLAYBOOK

DATE _____

M	TU	W	TH	F	SA	SU

MY **CELEBRATION** EXPERIENCE™

MY **GRATITUDE** EXPANDER™

MY **DAILY** INTENTION™

MY BEFORE **NOON** COMMITMENTS™

MY **TO-DO** GAMEPLAN™

MY **APPOINTMENT** TRACKER™

MY **NOTE** KEEPER™

MY **HABIT** TRANSFORMER™

MY **VISION** BOARD™

Review page 18–19

Love WATER

LIFE PURPOSE PLAYBOOK

M | TU | W | TH | F | SA | SU | DATE

MY **DAILY PAGE** PLATFORM™

MY **BEFORE NOON** COMMITMENTS™

MY **CELEBRATION** EXPERIENCE™

MY **GRATITUDE** EXPANDER™

MY **DAILY** INTENTION™

MY **TO-DO** GAMEPLAN™

MY **NOTE** KEEPER™

MY **APPOINTMENT** TRACKER™

MY **HABIT** TRANSFORMER™

MY **VISION** BOARD™

Review page 18–19

LoveWATER

LIFE PURPOSE PLAYBOOK

MY **WEEKLY** CELEBRATION EXPERIENCE™

MY **OVERFLOW** TASKS™

MY
LIFE VISION
REVIEW™

Add the dates to the next 7 pages of
MY DAILY PAGE PLATFORM™.

Now review the following sections of this playbook
& transfer any tasks or projects into those 7 pages.

Any that are not urgent for this week should be
scheduled into MY OVERFLOW TASKS
on the NEXT **WEEKLY CHECK-IN.**

MY LIFE INTENTION MATRIX™
(page 14)

MY CIRCLE OF LIFE EXPANDER™
(page 21)

MY GOAL CHARTING SYSTEM™
(page 24–25)

MY IDEA & PROJECT MAGNIFIER™
(page 26–27)

MY TO-DO CHECKLIST™
(page 28–29)

MY YEAR AHEAD OUTLOOK™
(page 31)

MY MONTHLY PLANNER™
(page 32–55)

MY 3 MUST-DO's THIS WEEK™

M   TU   W   TH   F   SA   SU   DATE _____

MY DAILY PAGE PLATFORM™

MY BEFORE NOON COMMITMENTS™

am

MY CELEBRATION EXPERIENCE™

MY GRATITUDE EXPANDER™

MY DAILY INTENTION™

MY TO-DO GAMEPLAN™

MY NOTE KEEPER™

MY APPOINTMENT TRACKER™

MY HABIT TRANSFORMER™

MY VISION BOARD™

Review page 18–19

Love WATER

LIFE PURPOSE PLAYBOOK

DATE _____ M TU W TH F SA SU

MY **CELEBRATION** EXPERIENCE™

MY **GRATITUDE** EXPANDER™

MY **DAILY** INTENTION™

MY **BEFORE NOON** COMMITMENTS™

MY **TO-DO** GAMEPLAN™

MY **APPOINTMENT** TRACKER™

MY **NOTE** KEEPER™

MY **HABIT** TRANSFORMER™

MY **VISION** BOARD™

Review page 18–19

LoveWATER

LIFE PURPOSE PLAYBOOK

M TU W TH F SA SU DATE _____

MY DAILY PAGE PLATFORM™

MY **BEFORE NOON** COMMITMENTS™

MY **CELEBRATION** EXPERIENCE™

MY **GRATITUDE** EXPANDER™

MY **DAILY** INTENTION™

MY **TO-DO** GAMEPLAN™

MY **NOTE** KEEPER™

MY **APPOINTMENT** TRACKER™

MY **HABIT** TRANSFORMER™

MY **VISION** BOARD™

Review page 18–19

LoveWATER

LIFE PURPOSE PLAYBOOK

DATE _____ | M | TU | W | TH | F | SA | SU |

MY **CELEBRATION** EXPERIENCE™

MY **GRATITUDE** EXPANDER™

MY **DAILY** INTENTION™

MY **TO-DO** GAMEPLAN™

MY BEFORE **NOON** COMMITMENTS™

MY **APPOINTMENT** TRACKER™

MY **NOTE** KEEPER™

MY **HABIT** TRANSFORMER™

MY **VISION** BOARD™

Review page 18–19

Love WATER

LIFE PURPOSE PLAYBOOK

M   TU   W   TH   F   SA   SU   DATE _____

MY DAILY PAGE PLATFORM™

MY *BEFORE NOON* COMMITMENTS™

MY *CELEBRATION* EXPERIENCE™

MY *GRATITUDE* EXPANDER™

MY *DAILY* INTENTION™

MY *TO-DO* GAMEPLAN™

····· MY *NOTE* KEEPER™ ·····

MY *APPOINTMENT* TRACKER™

MY *HABIT* TRANSFORMER™

MY *VISION* BOARD™

Review page 18–19

Love WATER

LIFE PURPOSE PLAYBOOK

DATE _____

| M | TU | W | TH | F | SA | SU |

MY **CELEBRATION** EXPERIENCE™

MY **GRATITUDE** EXPANDER™

MY **DAILY** INTENTION™

MY **TO-DO** GAMEPLAN™

MY BEFORE **NOON** COMMITMENTS™

MY **DAILY PAGE** PLATFORM™

MY **APPOINTMENT** TRACKER™

MY **NOTE** KEEPER™

MY **HABIT** TRANSFORMER™

MY **VISION** BOARD™

Review page 18–19

Love WATER

LIFE PURPOSE PLAYBOOK

M / TU / W / TH / F / SA / SU / DATE _____

MY **DAILY PAGE** PLATFORM™

MY **BEFORE NOON** COMMITMENTS™

MY **CELEBRATION** EXPERIENCE™

MY **GRATITUDE** EXPANDER™

MY **DAILY** INTENTION™

MY **TO-DO** GAMEPLAN™

MY **NOTE** KEEPER™

MY **APPOINTMENT** TRACKER™

MY **HABIT** TRANSFORMER™

MY **VISION** BOARD™

Review page 18–19

Love WATER

LIFE PURPOSE PLAYBOOK

MY **WEEKLY** CELEBRATION EXPERIENCE™

MY
OVERFLOW
TASKS™

MY
LIFE VISION
REVIEW™

Add the dates to the next 7 pages of
MY DAILY PAGE PLATFORM™.

Now review the following sections of this playbook
& transfer any tasks or projects into those 7 pages.

Any that are not urgent for this week should be
scheduled into MY OVERFLOW TASKS
on the NEXT **WEEKLY CHECK-IN.**

MY LIFE INTENTION MATRIX™
(page 14)

MY CIRCLE OF LIFE EXPANDER™
(page 21)

MY GOAL CHARTING SYSTEM™
(page 24–25)

MY IDEA & PROJECT MAGNIFIER™
(page 26–27)

MY TO-DO CHECKLIST™
(page 28–29)

MY YEAR AHEAD OUTLOOK™
(page 31)

MY MONTHLY PLANNER™
(page 32–55)

MY **3 MUST-DO's** THIS WEEK™

M TU W TH F SA SU DATE

MY **DAILY PAGE** PLATFORM™

MY *BEFORE NOON* COMMITMENTS™

am

MY **CELEBRATION** EXPERIENCE™

MY **GRATITUDE** EXPANDER™

MY **DAILY** INTENTION™

MY **TO-DO** GAMEPLAN™

MY **NOTE** KEEPER™

MY **APPOINTMENT** TRACKER™

MY **HABIT** TRANSFORMER™

MY **VISION** BOARD™

Review page 18—19

Love WATER

LIFE PURPOSE PLAYBOOK

DATE | M | TU | W | TH | F | SA | SU

MY **CELEBRATION** EXPERIENCE™

MY **GRATITUDE** EXPANDER™

MY **DAILY** INTENTION™

MY **TO-DO** GAMEPLAN™

MY BEFORE **NOON** COMMITMENTS™

MY **DAILY PAGE** PLATFORM™

MY **APPOINTMENT** TRACKER™

MY **NOTE** KEEPER™

MY **HABIT** TRANSFORMER™

MY **VISION** BOARD™

Review page 18–19

Love WATER

LIFE PURPOSE PLAYBOOK

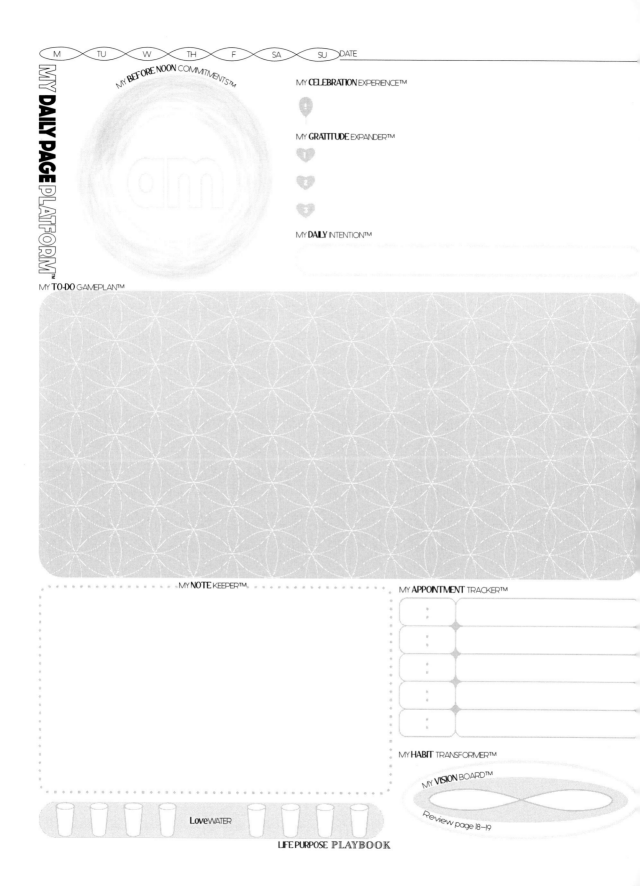

M | TU | W | TH | F | SA | SU | DATE

MY DAILY PAGE PLATFORM™

MY BEFORE NOON COMMITMENTS™

MY CELEBRATION EXPERIENCE™

MY GRATITUDE EXPANDER™

MY DAILY INTENTION™

MY TO-DO GAMEPLAN™

MY NOTE KEEPER™

MY APPOINTMENT TRACKER™

MY HABIT TRANSFORMER™

MY VISION BOARD™

Review page 18–19

LoveWATER

LIFE PURPOSE PLAYBOOK

DATE _____

MY **CELEBRATION** EXPERIENCE™

MY **GRATITUDE** EXPANDER™

MY **DAILY** INTENTION™

MY BEFORE **NOON** COMMITMENTS™

MY **DAILY PAGE** PLATFORM™

MY **TO-DO** GAMEPLAN™

MY **APPOINTMENT** TRACKER™

MY **NOTE** KEEPER™

MY **HABIT** TRANSFORMER™

MY **VISION** BOARD™

Review page 18–19

Love WATER

LIFE PURPOSE PLAYBOOK

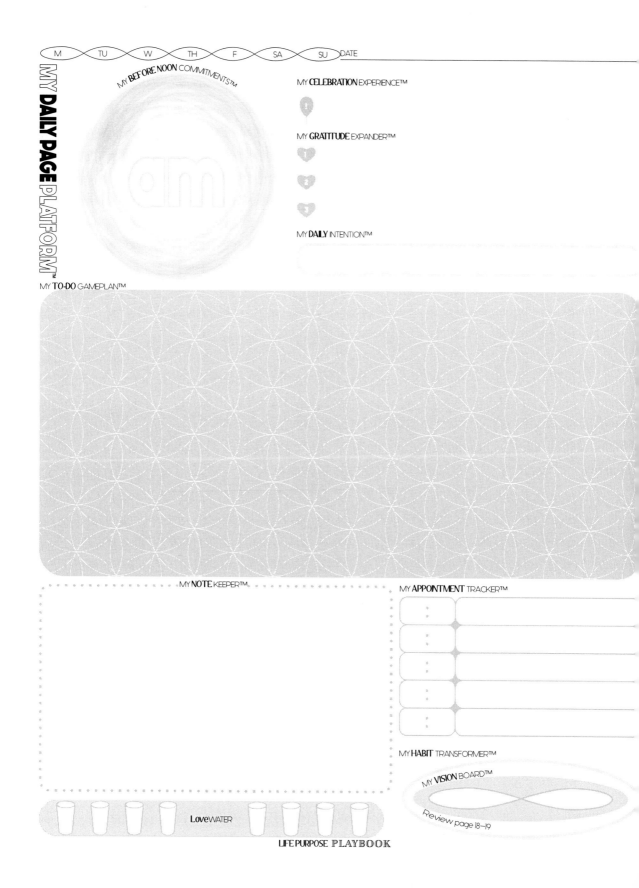

M   TU   W   TH   F   SA   SU   DATE _____

MY **DAILY PAGE** PLATFORM™

MY **BEFORE NOON** COMMITMENTS™

MY **CELEBRATION** EXPERIENCE™

MY **GRATITUDE** EXPANDER™

MY **DAILY** INTENTION™

MY **TO-DO** GAMEPLAN™

MY **NOTE** KEEPER™

MY **APPOINTMENT** TRACKER™

MY **HABIT** TRANSFORMER™

MY **VISION** BOARD™

Review page 18–19

Love WATER

LIFE PURPOSE PLAYBOOK

DATE _____

| M | TU | W | TH | F | SA | SU |

MY **CELEBRATION** EXPERIENCE™

MY BEFORE **NOON** COMMITMENTS™

MY **GRATITUDE** EXPANDER™

MY **DAILY** INTENTION™

MY **TO-DO** GAMEPLAN™

MY **APPOINTMENT** TRACKER™

MY **NOTE** KEEPER™

MY **HABIT** TRANSFORMER™

MY **VISION** BOARD™

Review page 18–19

Love WATER

LIFE PURPOSE PLAYBOOK

M | TU | W | TH | F | SA | SU | DATE _____

MY DAILY PAGE PLATFORM™

MY **BEFORE NOON** COMMITMENTS™

am

MY **CELEBRATION** EXPERIENCE™

MY **GRATITUDE** EXPANDER™

MY **DAILY** INTENTION™

MY **TO-DO** GAMEPLAN™

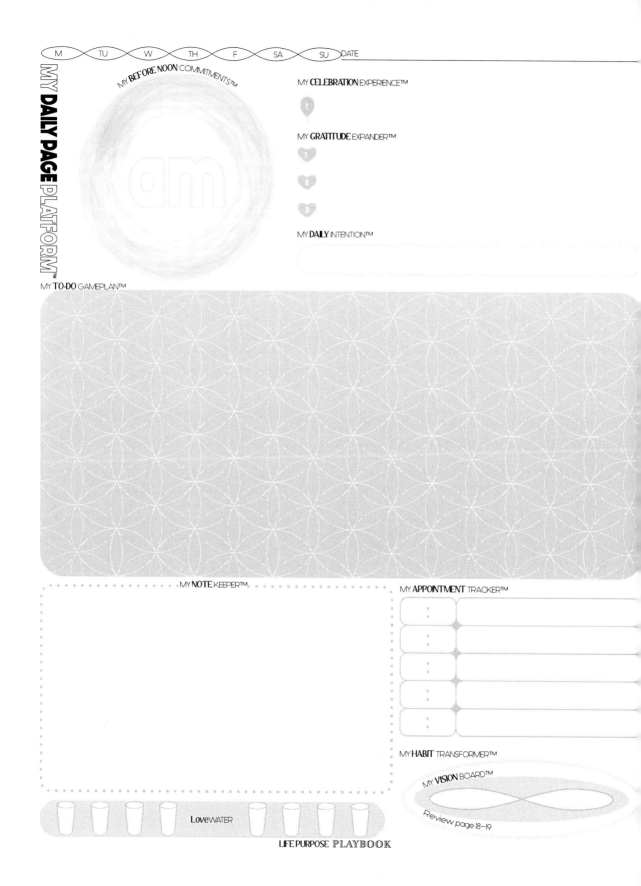

MY **NOTE** KEEPER™

MY **APPOINTMENT** TRACKER™

MY **HABIT** TRANSFORMER™

MY **VISION** BOARD™

Review page 18–19

LoveWATER

LIFE PURPOSE PLAYBOOK

MY **WEEKLY** CELEBRATION EXPERIENCE™

MY
OVERFLOW
TASKS™

MY
LIFE VISION
REVIEW™

Add the dates to the next 7 pages of
MY DAILY PAGE PLATFORM™.

Now review the following sections of this playbook
& transfer any tasks or projects into those 7 pages.

Any that are not urgent for this week should be
scheduled into MY OVERFLOW TASKS
on the NEXT **WEEKLY CHECK–IN.**

MY LIFE INTENTION MATRIX™
(page 14)

MY CIRCLE OF LIFE EXPANDER™
(page 21)

MY GOAL CHARTING SYSTEM™
(page 24–25)

MY IDEA & PROJECT MAGNIFIER™
(page 26–27)

MY TO–DO CHECKLIST™
(page 28–29)

MY YEAR AHEAD OUTLOOK™
(page 31)

MY MONTHLY PLANNER™
(page 32–55)

MY 3 MUST-DO'S THIS WEEK™

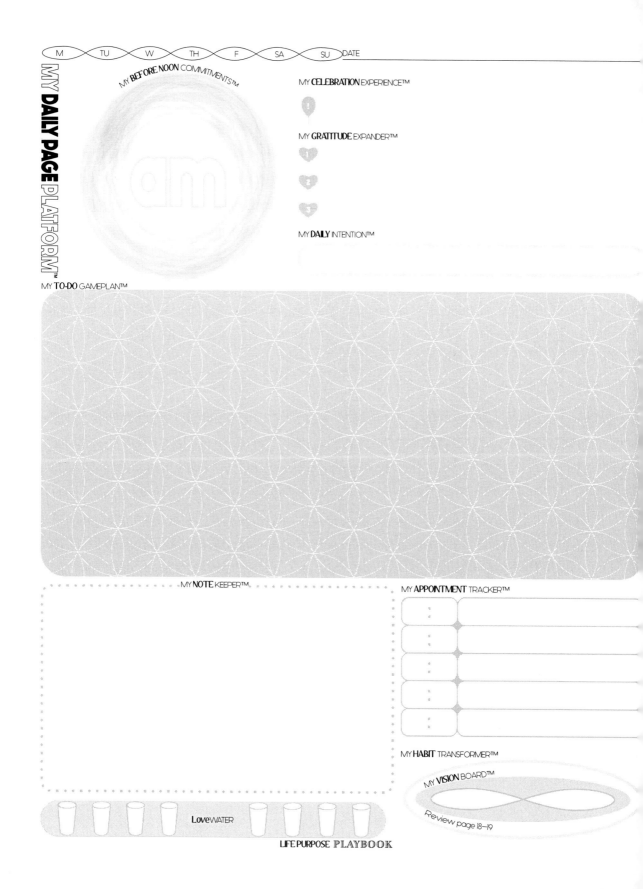

M | TU | W | TH | F | SA | SU | DATE

MY **DAILY PAGE** PLATFORM™

MY *BEFORE NOON* COMMITMENTS™

MY **CELEBRATION** EXPERIENCE™

MY **GRATITUDE** EXPANDER™

MY **DAILY** INTENTION™

MY **TO-DO** GAMEPLAN™

MY **NOTE** KEEPER™

MY **APPOINTMENT** TRACKER™

MY **HABIT** TRANSFORMER™

MY **VISION** BOARD™
Review page 18—19

Love WATER

LIFE PURPOSE PLAYBOOK

DATE _____ | M | TU | W | TH | F | SA | SU |

MY **CELEBRATION** EXPERIENCE™

MY **BEFORE NOON** COMMITMENTS™

MY **GRATITUDE** EXPANDER™

MY **DAILY** INTENTION™

MY **TO-DO** GAMEPLAN™

MY **APPOINTMENT** TRACKER™

MY **NOTE** KEEPER™

MY **HABIT** TRANSFORMER™

MY **VISION** BOARD™

Review page 18–19

Love WATER

LIFE PURPOSE PLAYBOOK

MY DAILY PAGE PLATFORM™

M TU W TH F SA SU DATE _____

MY DAILY PAGE PLATFORM™

MY **BEFORE NOON** COMMITMENTS™

MY **CELEBRATION** EXPERIENCE™

MY **GRATITUDE** EXPANDER™

MY **DAILY** INTENTION™

MY **TO-DO** GAMEPLAN™

MY **NOTE** KEEPER™

MY **APPOINTMENT** TRACKER™

MY **HABIT** TRANSFORMER™

MY **VISION** BOARD™

Review page 18–19

Love WATER

LIFE PURPOSE PLAYBOOK

DATE _____ M | TU | W | TH | F | SA | SU

MY **CELEBRATION** EXPERIENCE™

MY **BEFORE NOON** COMMITMENTS™

MY **GRATITUDE** EXPANDER™

MY **DAILY** INTENTION™

MY **TO-DO** GAMEPLAN™

MY **APPOINTMENT** TRACKER™

MY **NOTE** KEEPER™

MY **HABIT** TRANSFORMER™

MY **VISION** BOARD™

Review page 18–19

Love WATER

LIFE PURPOSE PLAYBOOK

MY DAILY PAGE PLATFORM™

MY **DAILY PAGE** PLATFORM™

MY **BEFORE NOON** COMMITMENTS™

MY **CELEBRATION** EXPERIENCE™

MY **GRATITUDE** EXPANDER™

1

2

3

MY **DAILY** INTENTION™

MY **TO-DO** GAMEPLAN™

MY **NOTE** KEEPER™

MY **APPOINTMENT** TRACKER™

MY **HABIT** TRANSFORMER™

MY **VISION** BOARD™

Review page 18–19

Love WATER

LIFE PURPOSE PLAYBOOK

DATE _____

M | TU | W | TH | F | SA | SU

MY **CELEBRATION** EXPERIENCE™

MY **GRATITUDE** EXPANDER™

MY **DAILY** INTENTION™

MY **TO-DO** GAMEPLAN™

MY BEFORE **NOON** COMMITMENTS™

MY **DAILY PAGE** PLATFORM™

MY **APPOINTMENT** TRACKER™

MY **NOTE** KEEPER™

MY **HABIT** TRANSFORMER™

MY **VISION** BOARD™

Review page 18–19

Love WATER

LIFE PURPOSE PLAYBOOK

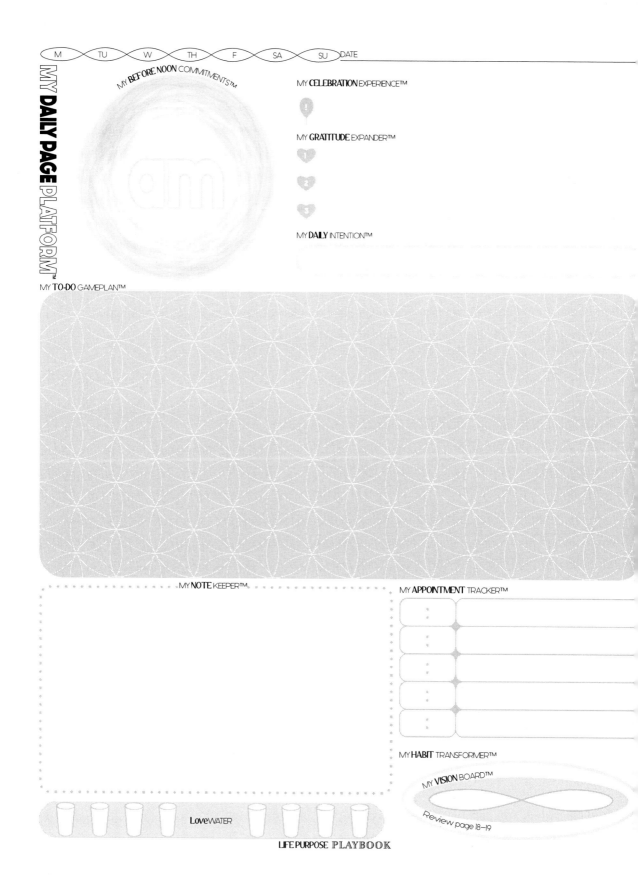

M | TU | W | TH | F | SA | SU | DATE

MY DAILY PAGE PLATFORM™

MY BEFORE NOON COMMITMENTS™

MY CELEBRATION EXPERIENCE™

MY GRATITUDE EXPANDER™

1

2

3

MY DAILY INTENTION™

MY TO-DO GAMEPLAN™

MY NOTE KEEPER™

MY APPOINTMENT TRACKER™

MY HABIT TRANSFORMER™

MY VISION BOARD™

Review page 18–19

Love WATER

LIFE PURPOSE PLAYBOOK

MY **WEEKLY** CELEBRATION EXPERIENCE™

MY
OVERFLOW
TASKS™

MY
LIFE VISION
REVIEW™

Add the dates to the next 7 pages of
MY DAILY PAGE PLATFORM™.

Now review the following sections of this playbook
& transfer any tasks or projects into those 7 pages

Any that are not urgent for this week should be
scheduled into MY OVERFLOW TASKS
on the NEXT **WEEKLY CHECK-IN.**

MY LIFE INTENTION MATRIX™
(page 14)

MY CIRCLE OF LIFE EXPANDER™
(page 21)

MY GOAL CHARTING SYSTEM™
(page 24–25)

MY IDEA & PROJECT MAGNIFIER™
(page 26–27)

MY TO-DO CHECKLIST™
(page 28–29)

MY YEAR AHEAD OUTLOOK™
(page 31)

MY MONTHLY PLANNER™
(page 32–55)

MY 3 MUST-DO'S THIS WEEK™

M | TU | W | TH | F | SA | SU | DATE _____

MY **DAILY** PAGE PLATFORM™

MY **BEFORE NOON** COMMITMENTS™

MY **CELEBRATION** EXPERIENCE™

MY **GRATITUDE** EXPANDER™

1

2

3

MY **DAILY** INTENTION™

MY **TO-DO** GAMEPLAN™

MY **NOTE** KEEPER™

MY **APPOINTMENT** TRACKER™

MY **HABIT** TRANSFORMER™

MY **VISION** BOARD™

Review page 18–19

Love WATER

LIFE PURPOSE PLAYBOOK

DATE _____

MY **CELEBRATION** EXPERIENCE™

MY BEFORE **NOON** COMMITMENTS™

MY **GRATITUDE** EXPANDER™

MY **DAILY** INTENTION™

MY **TO-DO** GAMEPLAN™

MY **APPOINTMENT** TRACKER™

MY **NOTE** KEEPER™

MY **HABIT** TRANSFORMER™

MY **VISION** BOARD™

Review page 18–19

Love WATER

LIFE PURPOSE PLAYBOOK

M | TU | W | TH | F | SA | SU | DATE _____

MY **DAILY PAGE** PLATFORM™

MY **BEFORE NOON** COMMITMENTS™

am

MY **CELEBRATION** EXPERIENCE™

MY **GRATITUDE** EXPANDER™

1

2

3

MY **DAILY** INTENTION™

MY **TO-DO** GAMEPLAN™

MY **NOTE** KEEPER™

MY **APPOINTMENT** TRACKER™

MY **HABIT** TRANSFORMER™

MY **VISION** BOARD™

Review page 18–19

Love WATER

LIFE PURPOSE PLAYBOOK

DATE _____

| M | TU | W | TH | F | SA | SU |

MY **CELEBRATION** EXPERIENCE™

MY **GRATITUDE** EXPANDER™

MY **DAILY** INTENTION™

MY **TO-DO** GAMEPLAN™

MY BEFORE **NOON** COMMITMENTS™

MY **DAILY PAGE** PLATFORM™

MY **APPOINTMENT** TRACKER™

MY **NOTE** KEEPER™

MY **HABIT** TRANSFORMER™

MY **VISION** BOARD™

Review page 18–19

Love WATER

LIFE PURPOSE PLAYBOOK

M | TU | W | TH | F | SA | SU | DATE

MY **DAILY PAGE** PLATFORM™

MY **BEFORE NOON** COMMITMENTS™

MY **CELEBRATION** EXPERIENCE™

MY **GRATITUDE** EXPANDER™

MY **DAILY** INTENTION™

MY **TO-DO** GAMEPLAN™

MY **NOTE** KEEPER™

MY **APPOINTMENT** TRACKER™

MY **HABIT** TRANSFORMER™

MY **VISION** BOARD™

Review page 18–19

LoveWATER

LIFE PURPOSE PLAYBOOK

DATE _____

| M | TU | W | TH | F | SA | SU |

MY **CELEBRATION** EXPERIENCE™

MY **BEFORE NOON** COMMITMENTS™

MY DAILY PAGE PLATFORM™

MY **GRATITUDE** EXPANDER™

MY **DAILY** INTENTION™

MY **TO-DO** GAMEPLAN™

MY **APPOINTMENT** TRACKER™

MY **NOTE** KEEPER™

MY **HABIT** TRANSFORMER™

MY **VISION** BOARD™

Review page 18–19

Love WATER

LIFE PURPOSE PLAYBOOK

MY **DAILY PAGE** PLATFORM™

MY **BEFORE NOON** COMMITMENTS™

MY **CELEBRATION** EXPERIENCE™

MY **GRATITUDE** EXPANDER™

MY **DAILY** INTENTION™

MY **TO-DO** GAMEPLAN™

MY **NOTE** KEEPER™

MY **APPOINTMENT** TRACKER™

MY **HABIT** TRANSFORMER™

MY **VISION** BOARD™

Review page 18–19

Love WATER

LIFE PURPOSE PLAYBOOK

MY WEEKLY CELEBRATION EXPERIENCE™

MY OVERFLOW TASKS™

MY
LIFE VISION
REVIEW™

Add the dates to the next 7 pages of
MY DAILY PAGE PLATFORM™.

Now review the following sections of this playbook
& transfer any tasks or projects into those 7 pages.

Any that are not urgent for this week should be
scheduled into MY OVERFLOW TASKS
on the NEXT **WEEKLY CHECK-IN.**

MY LIFE INTENTION MATRIX™
(page 14)

MY CIRCLE OF LIFE EXPANDER™
(page 21)

MY GOAL CHARTING SYSTEM™
(page 24–25)

MY IDEA & PROJECT MAGNIFIER™
(page 26–27)

MY TO-DO CHECKLIST™
(page 28–29)

MY YEAR AHEAD OUTLOOK™
(page 31)

MY MONTHLY PLANNER™
(page 32–55)

MY 3 MUST-DO'S THIS WEEK™

M | TU | W | TH | F | SA | SU | DATE _____

MY **DAILY PAGE** PLATFORM™

MY **BEFORE NOON** COMMITMENTS™

MY **CELEBRATION** EXPERIENCE™

MY **GRATITUDE** EXPANDER™

MY **DAILY** INTENTION™

MY **TO-DO** GAMEPLAN™

MY **NOTE** KEEPER™

MY **APPOINTMENT** TRACKER™

MY **HABIT** TRANSFORMER™

MY **VISION** BOARD™

Review page 18–19

Love WATER

LIFE PURPOSE PLAYBOOK

DATE _____ (M)(TU)(W)(TH)(F)(SA)(SU)

MY **CELEBRATION** EXPERIENCE™

MY **GRATITUDE** EXPANDER™

MY **DAILY** INTENTION™

MY **TO-DO** GAMEPLAN™

MY BEFORE **NOON** COMMITMENTS™

MY DAILY PAGE PLATFORM™

MY **APPOINTMENT** TRACKER™

MY **NOTE** KEEPER™

MY **HABIT** TRANSFORMER™

MY **VISION** BOARD™

Review page 18–19

Love WATER

LIFE PURPOSE PLAYBOOK

MY **DAILY PAGE** PLATFORM™

M TU W TH F SA SU DATE

MY **BEFORE NOON** COMMITMENTS™

MY **CELEBRATION** EXPERIENCE™

MY **GRATITUDE** EXPANDER™

MY **DAILY** INTENTION™

MY **TO-DO** GAMEPLAN™

MY **NOTE** KEEPER™

MY **APPOINTMENT** TRACKER™

MY **HABIT** TRANSFORMER™

MY **VISION** BOARD™

Review page 18—19

LoveWATER

LIFE PURPOSE PLAYBOOK

DATE _____

MY **CELEBRATION** EXPERIENCE™

MY **GRATITUDE** EXPANDER™

MY **DAILY** INTENTION™

MY **TO-DO** GAMEPLAN™

MY BEFORE **NOON** COMMITMENTS™

MY DAILY PAGE PLATFORM™

MY **APPOINTMENT** TRACKER™

MY **NOTE** KEEPER™

MY **HABIT** TRANSFORMER™

MY **VISION** BOARD™

Review page 18–19

Love WATER

LIFE PURPOSE PLAYBOOK

M | TU | W | TH | F | SA | SU | DATE _____

MY DAILY PAGE PLATFORM™

MY *BEFORE NOON* COMMITMENTS™

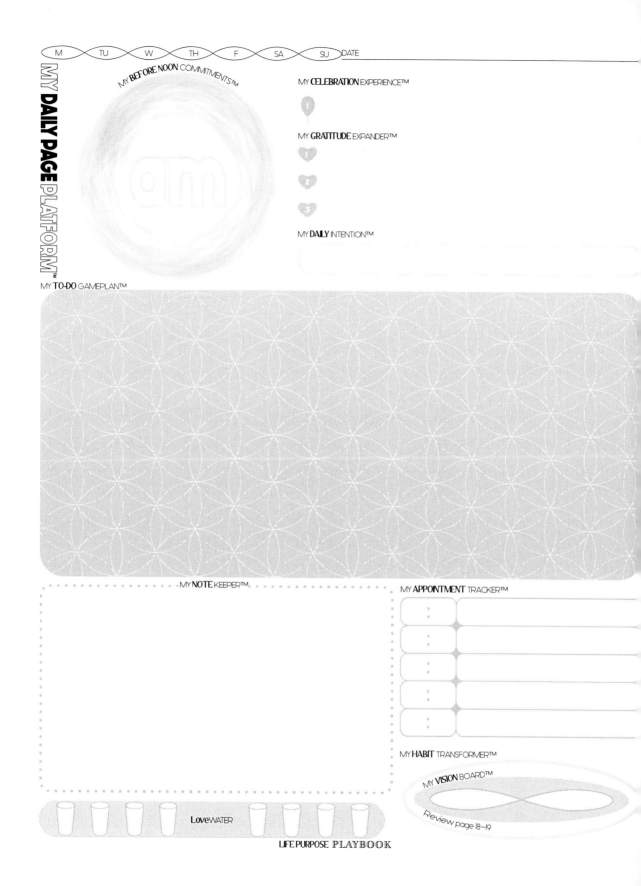

MY **CELEBRATION** EXPERIENCE™

MY **GRATITUDE** EXPANDER™

1
2
3

MY **DAILY** INTENTION™

MY **TO-DO** GAMEPLAN™

MY **NOTE** KEEPER™

MY **APPOINTMENT** TRACKER™

MY **HABIT** TRANSFORMER™

MY **VISION** BOARD™

Review page 18—19

Love WATER

LIFE PURPOSE PLAYBOOK

DATE _____ | M | TU | W | TH | F | SA | SU

MY **CELEBRATION** EXPERIENCE™

MY **GRATITUDE** EXPANDER™

MY **DAILY** INTENTION™

MY **TO-DO** GAMEPLAN™

MY BEFORE **NOON** COMMITMENTS™

MY **DAILY PAGE** PLATFORM™

MY **APPOINTMENT** TRACKER™

MY **NOTE** KEEPER™

MY **HABIT** TRANSFORMER™

MY **VISION** BOARD™

Review page 18–19

LoveWATER

LIFE PURPOSE PLAYBOOK

M / TU / W / TH / F / SA / SU / DATE _____

MY **DAILY PAGE** PLATFORM™

MY *BEFORE NOON* COMMITMENTS™

am

MY **CELEBRATION** EXPERIENCE™

MY **GRATITUDE** EXPANDER™

MY **DAILY** INTENTION™

MY **TO-DO** GAMEPLAN™

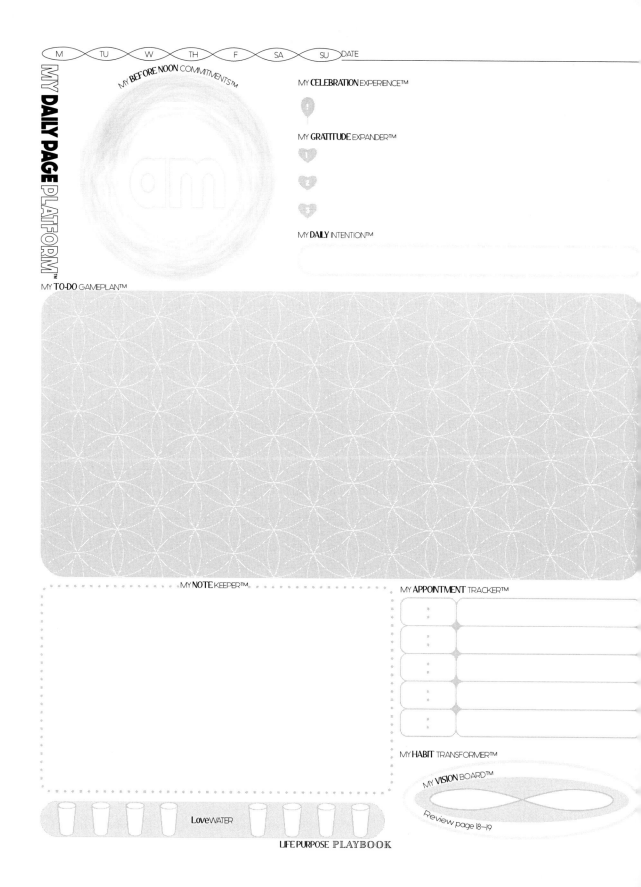

MY **NOTE** KEEPER™

MY **APPOINTMENT** TRACKER™

MY **HABIT** TRANSFORMER™

MY **VISION** BOARD™

Review page 18–19

Love WATER

LIFE PURPOSE **PLAYBOOK**

MY WEEKLY CELEBRATION EXPERIENCE™

MY OVERFLOW TASKS™

MY
LIFE VISION
REVIEW™

Add the dates to the next 7 pages of
MY DAILY PAGE PLATFORM™.

Now review the following sections of this playbook
& transfer any tasks or projects into those 7 pages.

Any that are not urgent for this week should be
scheduled into MY OVERFLOW TASKS
on the NEXT **WEEKLY CHECK-IN.**

MY LIFE INTENTION MATRIX™
(page 14)

MY CIRCLE OF LIFE EXPANDER™
(page 21)

MY GOAL CHARTING SYSTEM™
(page 24–25)

MY IDEA & PROJECT MAGNIFIER™
(page 26–27)

MY TO-DO CHECKLIST™
(page 28–29)

MY YEAR AHEAD OUTLOOK™
(page 31)

MY MONTHLY PLANNER™
(page 32–55)

MY 3 MUST-DO'S THIS WEEK™

M TU W TH F SA SU DATE

MY **DAILY PAGE** PLATFORM™

MY **BEFORE NOON** COMMITMENTS™

MY **CELEBRATION** EXPERIENCE™

MY **GRATITUDE** EXPANDER™

MY **DAILY** INTENTION™

MY **TO-DO** GAMEPLAN™

MY **NOTE** KEEPER™

MY **APPOINTMENT** TRACKER™

MY **HABIT** TRANSFORMER™

MY **VISION** BOARD™

Review page 18–19

LoveWATER

LIFE PURPOSE PLAYBOOK

DATE _____ M TU W TH F SA SU

MY **CELEBRATION** EXPERIENCE™

MY **GRATITUDE** EXPANDER™

MY **DAILY** INTENTION™

MY **TO-DO** GAMEPLAN™

MY BEFORE **NOON** COMMITMENTS™

MY **APPOINTMENT** TRACKER™

MY **NOTE** KEEPER™

MY **HABIT** TRANSFORMER™

MY **VISION** BOARD™

Review page 18–19

Love WATER

LIFE PURPOSE PLAYBOOK

M | TU | W | TH | F | SA | SU | DATE

MY **DAILY PAGE** PLATFORM™

MY **BEFORE NOON** COMMITMENTS™

am

MY **CELEBRATION** EXPERIENCE™

MY **GRATITUDE** EXPANDER™

MY **DAILY** INTENTION™

MY **TO-DO** GAMEPLAN™

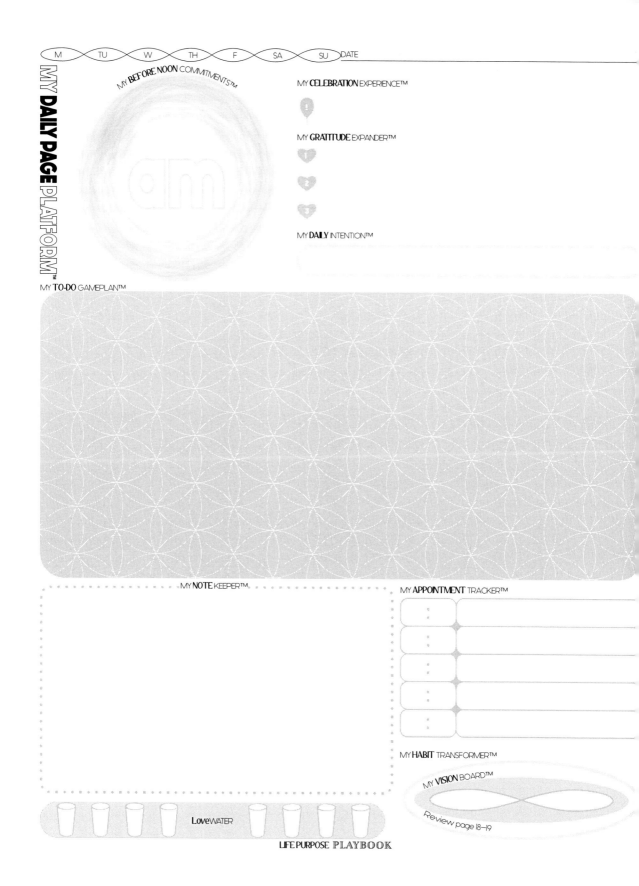

MY **NOTE** KEEPER™

MY **APPOINTMENT** TRACKER™

MY **HABIT** TRANSFORMER™

MY **VISION** BOARD™

Review page 18–19

Love WATER

LIFE PURPOSE PLAYBOOK

DATE _____

M TU W TH F SA SU

MY **CELEBRATION** EXPERIENCE™

MY **GRATITUDE** EXPANDER™

MY **DAILY** INTENTION™

MY BEFORE **NOON** COMMITMENTS™

MY **TO-DO** GAMEPLAN™

MY **APPOINTMENT** TRACKER™

MY **NOTE** KEEPER™

MY **HABIT** TRANSFORMER™

MY **VISION** BOARD™

Review page 18–19

Love WATER

LIFE PURPOSE PLAYBOOK

M TU W TH F SA SU DATE _____

MY DAILY PAGE PLATFORM™

MY **BEFORE NOON** COMMITMENTS™

am

MY **CELEBRATION** EXPERIENCE™

MY **GRATITUDE** EXPANDER™

MY **DAILY** INTENTION™

MY **TO-DO** GAMEPLAN™

MY **NOTE** KEEPER™

MY **APPOINTMENT** TRACKER™

MY **HABIT** TRANSFORMER™

MY **VISION** BOARD™

Review page 18–19

Love WATER

LIFE PURPOSE PLAYBOOK

DATE _____ | M | TU | W | TH | F | SA | SU |

MY **CELEBRATION** EXPERIENCE™

MY **GRATITUDE** EXPANDER™

MY **DAILY** INTENTION™

MY **TO-DO** GAMEPLAN™

MY **APPOINTMENT** TRACKER™

MY **HABIT** TRANSFORMER™

MY **VISION** BOARD™

Review page 18–19

MY BEFORE **NOON** COMMITMENTS™

MY **DAILY PAGE** PLATFORM™

MY **NOTE** KEEPER™

Love WATER

LIFE PURPOSE PLAYBOOK

M | TU | W | TH | F | SA | SU | DATE _____

MY DAILY PAGE PLATFORM™

MY **BEFORE NOON** COMMITMENTS™

MY **CELEBRATION** EXPERIENCE™

MY **GRATITUDE** EXPANDER™

MY **DAILY** INTENTION™

MY **TO-DO** GAMEPLAN™

MY **NOTE** KEEPER™

MY **APPOINTMENT** TRACKER™

MY **HABIT** TRANSFORMER™

MY **VISION** BOARD™

Review page 18–19

Love WATER

LIFE PURPOSE PLAYBOOK

MY WEEKLY CELEBRATION EXPERIENCE™

MY OVERFLOW TASKS™

MY LIFE VISION REVIEW™

Add the dates to the next 7 pages of
MY DAILY PAGE PLATFORM™.

Now review the following sections of this playbook
& transfer any tasks or projects into those 7 pages

Any that are not urgent for this week should be
scheduled into MY OVERFLOW TASKS
on the NEXT **WEEKLY CHECK-IN.**

MY LIFE INTENTION MATRIX™
(page 14)

MY CIRCLE OF LIFE EXPANDER™
(page 21)

MY GOAL CHARTING SYSTEM™
(page 24–25)

MY IDEA & PROJECT MAGNIFIER™
(page 26–27)

MY TO-DO CHECKLIST™
(page 28–29)

MY YEAR AHEAD OUTLOOK™
(page 31)

MY MONTHLY PLANNER™
(page 32–55)

MY 3 MUST-DO'S THIS WEEK™

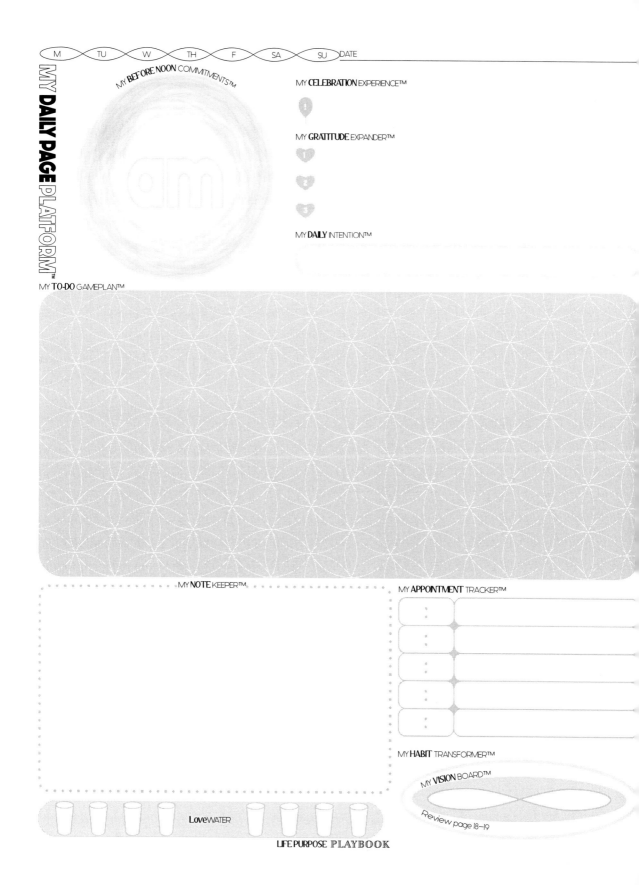

M TU W TH F SA SU DATE _____

MY **DAILY PAGE** PLATFORM™

MY **BEFORE NOON** COMMITMENTS™

MY **CELEBRATION** EXPERIENCE™

MY **GRATITUDE** EXPANDER™

1

2

3

MY **DAILY** INTENTION™

MY **TO-DO** GAMEPLAN™

MY **NOTE** KEEPER™

MY **APPOINTMENT** TRACKER™

MY **HABIT** TRANSFORMER™

MY **VISION** BOARD™

Review page 18–19

Love WATER

LIFE PURPOSE PLAYBOOK

DATE _____

| M | TU | W | TH | F | SA | SU |

MY **CELEBRATION** EXPERIENCE™

MY BEFORE **NOON** COMMITMENTS™

MY **GRATITUDE** EXPANDER™

MY **DAILY** INTENTION™

MY **DAILY PAGE** PLATFORM™

MY **TO-DO** GAMEPLAN™

MY **APPOINTMENT** TRACKER™

MY **NOTE** KEEPER™

MY **HABIT** TRANSFORMER™

MY **VISION** BOARD™

Review page 18–19

Love WATER

LIFE PURPOSE PLAYBOOK

MY **DAILY PAGE** PLATFORM™

MY **BEFORE NOON** COMMITMENTS™

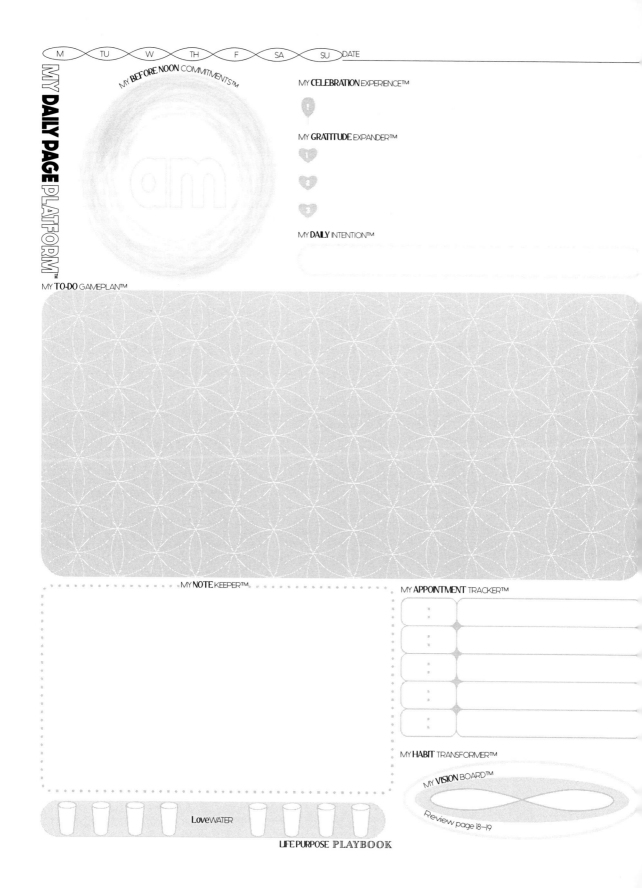

MY **CELEBRATION** EXPERIENCE™

MY **GRATITUDE** EXPANDER™

MY **DAILY** INTENTION™

MY **TO-DO** GAMEPLAN™

MY **NOTE** KEEPER™

MY **APPOINTMENT** TRACKER™

MY **HABIT** TRANSFORMER™

MY **VISION** BOARD™

Review page 18-19

Love WATER

LIFE PURPOSE PLAYBOOK

MY CELEBRATION EXPERIENCE™

MY GRATITUDE EXPANDER™

MY DAILY INTENTION™

MY TO-DO GAMEPLAN™

MY BEFORE NOON COMMITMENTS™

MY APPOINTMENT TRACKER™

MY NOTE KEEPER™

MY HABIT TRANSFORMER™

MY VISION BOARD™

Review page 18–19

Love WATER

M / TU / W / TH / F / SA / SU / DATE _____

MY DAILY PAGE PLATFORM™

MY **BEFORE NOON** COMMITMENTS™

MY **CELEBRATION** EXPERIENCE™

MY **GRATITUDE** EXPANDER™

MY **DAILY** INTENTION™

MY **TO-DO** GAMEPLAN™

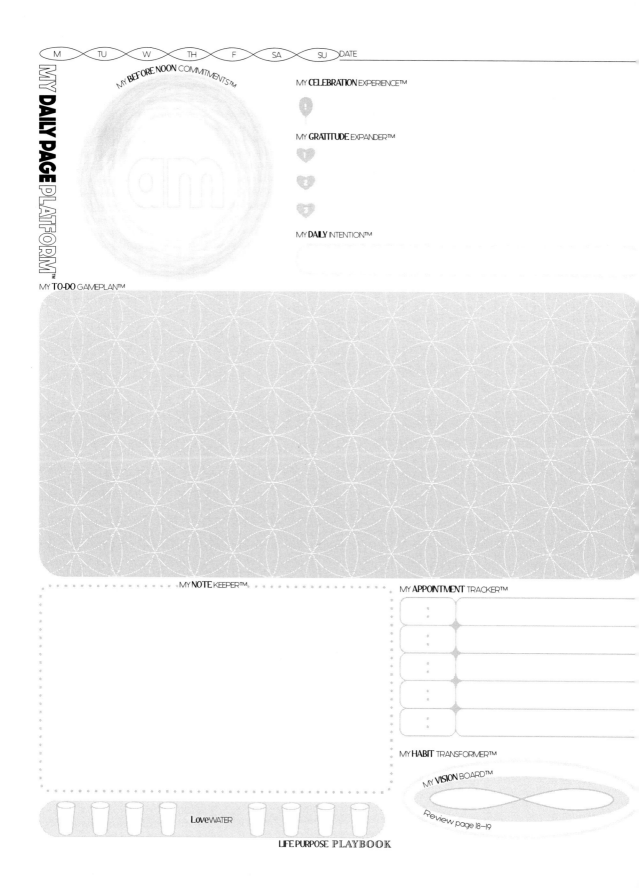

MY **NOTE** KEEPER™

MY **APPOINTMENT** TRACKER™

MY **HABIT** TRANSFORMER™

MY **VISION** BOARD™

Review page 18-19

Love WATER

LIFE PURPOSE PLAYBOOK

MY **CELEBRATION** EXPERIENCE™

MY BEFORE **NOON** COMMITMENTS™

MY DAILY PAGE PLATFORM™

MY **GRATITUDE** EXPANDER™

MY **DAILY** INTENTION™

MY **TO-DO** GAMEPLAN™

MY **APPOINTMENT** TRACKER™

MY **NOTE** KEEPER™

MY **HABIT** TRANSFORMER™

MY **VISION** BOARD™

Review page 18–19

Love WATER

LIFE PURPOSE PLAYBOOK

M   TU   W   TH   F   SA   SU   DATE

MY **DAILY PAGE** PLATFORM™

MY **BEFORE NOON** COMMITMENTS™

MY **CELEBRATION** EXPERIENCE™

MY **GRATITUDE** EXPANDER™

MY **DAILY** INTENTION™

MY **TO-DO** GAMEPLAN™

MY **NOTE** KEEPER™

MY **APPOINTMENT** TRACKER™

MY **HABIT** TRANSFORMER™

MY **VISION** BOARD™

Review page 18–19

Love WATER

LIFE PURPOSE PLAYBOOK

MY WEEKLY CELEBRATION EXPERIENCE™

MY OVERFLOW TASKS™

MY
LIFE VISION
REVIEW™

Add the dates to the next 7 pages of
MY DAILY PAGE PLATFORM™.

Now review the following sections of this playbook
& transfer any tasks or projects into those 7 pages.

Any that are not urgent for this week should be
scheduled into MY OVERFLOW TASKS
on the NEXT **WEEKLY CHECK-IN.**

MY LIFE INTENTION MATRIX™
(page 14) ⬤

MY CIRCLE OF LIFE EXPANDER™
(page 21) ⬤

MY GOAL CHARTING SYSTEM™
(page 24–25) ⬤

MY IDEA & PROJECT MAGNIFIER™
(page 26–27) ⬤

MY TO-DO CHECKLIST™
(page 28–29) ⬤

MY YEAR AHEAD OUTLOOK™
(page 31) ⬤

MY MONTHLY PLANNER™
(page 32–55) ⬤

MY **3 MUST-DO's** THIS WEEK™

THE GREATEST BENEFIT ISN`T GETTING WHAT YOU WANT.

THE GREATEST BENEFIT IS WHAT YOU`LL NEED TO BECOME IN ORDER TO GET WHAT YOU WANT.

THE JOURNEY IS EVERYTHING

ERIC WORRE

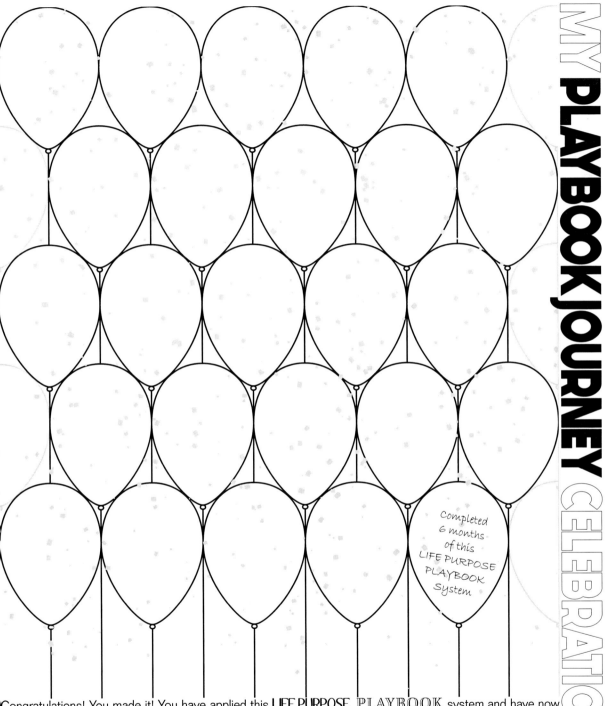

Completed
6 months
of this
LIFE PURPOSE
PLAYBOOK
System

Congratulations! You made it! You have applied this LIFE PURPOSE PLAYBOOK system and have now created some empowering habits for yourself! You've transformed, in many ways, and now you can look back at all of your achievements and be so incredibly proud of yourself! Take some time now to smile and write 24 achievements (big and small) from the past 6 months since using this LIFE PURPOSE PLAYBOOK. To continue your journey of personal transformation, visit **www.lifepurposeplaybook.com** and order another copy of this LIFE PURPOSE PLAYBOOK.

273

MY EXTRA SPACE™

274

Use this SPACE to take important notes, write out reference websites or favorite quotes, or even to doodle!

MY EXTRA SPACE™

276